About the author

Glen Humphries has been a journalist with the *Illawarra Mercury* for a long, long time. In that time he's seen the city change and has developed an interest in its history. He believes history doesn't have to be boring. For him the best histories are collections of stories that open our eyes to a place in a different way. He has written about Wollongong's history in the pages of the *Mercury*, including a daily column, as well as a trilogy of books about its music scene. He has gotten addicted to flicking through old local newspapers on the wonderful Trove website and knows how quickly you can end up down the rabbit hole. He goes on looking for one specific story and then ends up reading a load of articles from 1931 on some completely different subject. *Keira Street* is his 16th book and he honestly has no idea how he came to write that many. In fact, just now he had to go over to his book shelf and count all the titles twice because that number just seemed too high. He has a strong preference to wear trackpants while at home – and has been known to go to the shops without changing out of them. The second toe on both of his feet points away from the big toe – though he doesn't know why. If he enters a bookstore and leaves empty-handed he feels something is not quite right. Though he has to do that sometimes because even he knows he already owns far too many books. He's hoping that, once he retires, he'll have enough time to get through them all. At the bottom of the 'about the author' section of some of his books, he includes the mention that people should get in touch via email or social media with the phrase 'scooter party'. Just as a measure to see how many people actually read all the way to the bottom. Surprisingly to him some people do, as he has received a few 'scooter party' responses. So let's stick with that idea, okay? Send him a message - it'll be a little in-joke between you and him.

Published by Gelding Street Press
Aussie Rock Anthems: The Stories Behind Our Biggest Hit Songs
Sticky Wickets: Australian Cricket's Controversies and Curiosities
Jack Gibson's Fur Coat: Rugby League Oddities and Artefacts
Biff: Rugby League's Infamous Fights

Published by Last Day of School and available at www.lastdayofschool.net
Friday Night at the Oxford
Healer: The Rise, Fall and Return of Tumbleweed
Lull City: The Wollongong Music Scene 1955-2020
Alive in the Five: The Steelers' 1992 Premiership Charge
The Slab: 24 Stories of Beer in Australia
James Squire: The Biography
Sounds Like an Ending: Midnight Oil, 10-1 and Red Sails in the Sunset
Alright!: Queen at Live Aid
Little Darling: Daryl Braithwaite and The Horses
The Six-Pack: Stories from the World of Beer
Beer is Fun
Night Terrors: The True Story of the Kingsgrove Slasher

Keira Street

Glen Humphries

Last Day of School

ISBN: 978-0-6489911-6-8
Keira Street is copyright Glen Humphries 2024

For more information email dragstermag@hotmail.com. If you loved this book so much that you want to buy some more copies then head over to my micropublishing site Last Day of School (find it at www.lastdayofschool.net). And maybe buy some copies of my other books. They're good, I promise you. And all so reasonably priced.

This book is copyright. All rights reserved. Except for private study, research, criticism or reviews, as permitted under the Copyright Act, no part of this book may be reproduced, stored in a retrieval system, or transmitted in any form or by any means without prior written permission. That's not too much to ask, is it? Though I guess you don't need to be told that. If you're so interested in this book that you've gone to the trouble of reading the fine print on the copyright page, I'm sure you'll do the right thing.

Nobody knows what was here five minutes ago, just before they got here, let alone a hundred years.

Brooklyn Crime Novel
Jonathan Lethem

Keira Street

Introduction

Every street in the city has its stories, some have many, others only a few. The stretch of Keira Street between Smith and Burelli streets has seen plenty in its time, thanks to a combination of being one of the oldest streets in the city and a long-running major commercial street.

On a personal level my memories of Keira Street start with seeing a university friend playing gigs at the Illawarra Hotel in 1990. Growing up in Sydney, I only started to explore Wollongong when I started uni here. After those gigs were finished, there were a few options. One was a walk just up the road to Tamir Erkan's pizza shop on the western side of Keira Street, which was next-door to the original Food World Gourmet Café, which was in turn next to Cousins nightclub. That none of these places still exist in these location just goes to show how much Keira Street keeps moving. Erkan's served Turkish pizza, something that was unusual to many in Wollongong in 1990. But it was delicious and no Turkish pizza I've had since has touched it.

If more beer after the Illawarra was in order, then it tended to be a short stroll south along Keira Street to the Manhattan nightclub. It was buried deep in the guts of a dull-looking office block, with an entrance right about where His Boy Elroy and Schnitz sits. There were only two reasons to go there; it was open after the pubs closed and it had the novelty of phones in every booth, so you could ring someone sitting at another table.

When I got older and became a CBD worker, I'd frequently find myself in Keira Street, browsing or grabbing some lunch – maybe at Trang, who sponsored an indoor soccer team I played on (and by "sponsored" I mean gave us some shirts they'd found in a box out the back and didn't need any more).

So I got to see the ever-changing face of the street. And the changes happened so frequently that sometimes a freshly demolished block would appear, looking like a missing tooth in a smile, and I'd struggle to remember what was once there (if only we had Google Street View decades ago).

But there have been lots of other stories along Keira Street. It has seen plenty of action, including murder, arson and a gun-happy nightwatchman. Businesses have come and gone from the strip – including a funeral parlour, a car yard or two and even a petrol station. It is a key marker for an iconic family-owned bus company and a former football player who opened up multiple venues in the street's restaurant precinct. Bigger buildings have gone up, turning what was once a place where people lived to one where they work, shop and have fun

Keira Street

after hours.

The street was one of the first in the city, making it almost 200 years old. Charles Throsby Smith owned the land, living in a house down on Harbour Street. In 1834 he asked the government to send down a surveyor to lay out the township – presumably so CT Smith could then sell off his land in lots. That surveyor drew out a big rectangular block; bordered by Harbour, Crown, Keira and Smith streets with the hill at Market Square in the centre.

Of those four streets, Keira was the only one whose name reflected the First Nations people that walked the land long before the streets were mapped out. The name Keira comes from the white man's spelling of the mountain that could once be seen from the street but now only peeks through the gaps in the buildings.

The Wodi Wodi people of the Dharawal know that mountain as Djeera and its creation story is tied in with the Five Islands off the coast. Oola-boolo-woo was the West Wind and he had six daughters, Mimosa, Wilga, Lilli Pilli, Wattle, Clematis and Djerra, all living on top of the escarpment.

As his children misbehaved, Ool-boolo-woo cast them and the stone beneath them out to sea, forming the Five Islands. This left Djeera alone with no-one to play with; so she sat on the escarpment hunched over, staring out at her sisters. Eventually, she turned to stone and became part of the escarpment.

Initially, Keira Street sat on what seems to be a plateau, ending where the downward slopes began at Crown and

Smith streets, it was gradually lengthened. It seems the northward expansion came first, albeit with an odd five-legged intersection at Keira, Smith and Flinders streets. Odd because, over time it would make it impossible to drive the length of Keira Street, turning that northern section into what is in reality a completely separate road. Later, as the city grew to the south, Keira Street stretched out and became even longer.

That growth of the street would surely have had some effect on the street numbering of homes and businesses. In the early days the city was small enough not to bother with numbers; in newspaper ads one business would describe itself as being next to some other, well-known, business to help customers find them. Later, as the street lengthened first north and then south, street numbering became more necessary. And the numbering seems to have been reassigned as the street grew longer.

I have done my best to ensure that events included here actually happened in the blocks between Smith and Burelli streets, which has meant the need to overlook some interesting stories – such as the city council wanting to build an underground car park at MacCabe Park. But I did blur the boundaries a little to include some stories; if you could stand on either end of this section of Keira Street and see the spot where something happened it was allowed in. After all, while the mall isn't on Keira Street, the closure to traffic that occurred after its construction undeniably had an effect.

The aim with this book wasn't to create a deep and complete history of Keira Street, but to tell stories of

Keira Street

what happened along it, which is why the stories don't appear in chronological order (and the best histories are really collections of stories). It looks to show who walked the footpaths, who drove the streets, the ghosts of buildings now long gone. Hopefully, once you've finished the book, you'll walk the street and know what once happened on the corner on which you stand.

The Athena Club

George Skouras was sick of it. He'd been going to the club for years and all they seemed to do was cheat him out of his money. He'd had enough and so on the night of Thursday, September 6, he got his revenge.

The venue in question was the Athena Club upstairs on the southeastern corner of Keira and Crown streets. At about 7.45pm the club was full when someone smelled smoke and soon people were running from the flames. Some made their way out onto an awning, where they were saved by a Keira Street fruit merchant by the name of E Walker. He drove his truck under the awning and helped the people climb down onto it and away to safety.

Chris Kynesos wasn't quite so lucky, he jumped from a window and fractured his foot when he landed. Another member, George Mitchell (with the interesting job description of "potato merchant") made his way outside only to realise he'd left his jacket behind with the earnings from a hard day of potato selling in the pocket.

"I was just sitting down when the next minute the club

was in flames," Mitchell said. After the fire was out, he was able to return the club and find both his jacket and his potato money.

Christopher Bados, another member in the club at the time, insisted the fire had started in the kitchen and must have been from an electrical fault, because nothing but coffee and tea were being made at the time.

But it wasn't an electrical fault. It was the 22-year-old Skouras getting some of his own back. It was a pretty open and shut case; police had charged him with arson the very next day.

When the case came to court a week later (the law worked fast in those days) it became clear that Skouras wasn't interesting in being subtle. Athena Club co-owner Leo Paragois testified that he'd seen Skouras carrying a plastic can of petrol up the stairs of the club.

When he made it to the top of those stairs, Paragois said he saw Skouras pour the petrol on the floor and light a match before anyone could stop him. The co-owner then said he jumped over the flames and chased Skouras down the stairs and out of the club.

Skouras, who pleaded guilty to the fire, said the source of his anger was being cheated at card games at the club for the last three years.

On the night of the fire, Skouras had managed to lose his week's wages on a card game and asked Arthur Boyiatzis, the Athena Club's other owner, for a loan of £5. The owner refused, apparently because Skouras already owed him £5.

Skouras didn't take the refusal well. "Then I tell him I am going to close the place down and he hit me straight in the face," Skouras claimed. Boyiatzis instead claimed Skouras began swearing and throwing chairs around the club. Then, a half-hour later, he saw the flames.

The *Mercury* didn't record the sentence Skouras received, though he didn't seem to dispute they he lit the fire.

Keira kebabs

The humble kebab is synonymous with night-time dining. Late-night dining especially. Plenty of people have left a pub at midnight or later with a hankering for sliced meat, hoummos and tabouli. Plenty of those people had probably never eaten a kebab while the sun was up – but at night? Well, it just makes sense.

Except in Keira Street of course. With the blocks between Crown and Smith streets developing a reputation as a fine dining strip by the early 2000s, why would anyone think the place needed a kebab van?

Well, Wollongong City councillors did, allowing one to set up in a vacant block of land at 155 Keira Street opposite what was then Bourbon Street and right next door to L'Ambiance Seafood restaurant.

Unsurprisingly, restaurant manager Sandie Lysandrou was most unimpressed. "A lot of these people have spent money upgrading their shops and now council is putting a caravan in? It's like putting a kebab van in front of the Opera House."

Andrew Harper, who managed the Captain Snooze which would be neighbours with the kebab van, was also unimpressed. "Do we want to encourage tourism in this town or just a backward mentality?" he asked.

The councillors had allowed the kebab van to operate Wednesday-Saturday until 2am, with a range of conditions including providing lighting, toilets, chairs and tables as well as setting up the van at the rear of the block.

In their approval, not only did the councillors ignore the objections of nearby businesses, they also paid no attention to the fact the police thought it was a really, really bad idea.

"We've got three late-night trading licenced premises there," said Wollongong Police licencing officer Rob Tschentscher, "two of which close at 3am and another which operates 24 hours.

"This is also where a majority of people end up at the end of Friday and Saturday nights. The kebab van just gives people a legitimate excuse to stay there even longer."

Aside from the Labor councillors who had used their numbers to get the kebab van over the line, the only person in favour seemed to be Nick Manias. In a letter to the *Mercury*, he said he couldn't understand what the fuss was all about. "In contrast to the perceptions of the media and the concerned public, the proposed kebab van will improve the tourist image of the street," Manias wrote. And it was surely just a coincidence that he worked as a chef in the restaurant of Labor Lord Mayor George Harrison.

Keira Street

For some, it was that Labor dominance in the council that explained the curious decision to allow a kebab van in the city's main restaurant strip. You see, the man behind the kebab van was Zeki Esen, president of the ALP's Warrawong branch. And one of the Labor councillors was Kiril Jonovski, the secretary of that same branch. So when Lord Mayor Harrison claimed "I doubt if the majority of the caucus even know this man" it was hard to imagine he really expected anyone to believe him.

The protests that it wasn't simply a case of helping out a Labor mate totally collapsed when caucus member Violet Pocock broke ranks. She said that's exactly what was. "Maybe I am in the wrong political party," Pocock said. "He was obviously favoured by his connections. I am very pissed off about it. I had a really bad feeling about it. I have been railroaded."

Hours before the vote, Pocock was so concerned she said she rang Labor head office to work out how to balance her conscience and party responsibilities. But they did not call back in time and so she had to vote with the rest of the Labor caucus.

"I felt morally obligated to oppose it but I couldn't because of the threats that had been made," she said. Those threats – about being kicked off the council and out of the party – allegedly came from Harrison and Jonovski. Both of whom denied doing any such thing.

Then independent councillor Carolyn Griffiths planned to file a rescission motion over the kebab van decision. "To compromise the amenity of this strip of restaurants with a caravan and portaloos is beyond my comprehension," Griffiths said.

Fellow independent Pat Franks said it was time to go back and start all over again. "Now that Cr Pocock's claims have come out I think the whole situation should go back into the melting point [sic] and start again. I generally think that if you have the numbers you do the job but Cr Pocock's claims have made me re-think the issue."

All of this happened in the week after the decision. At the end of the week, Esen – who had been on holiday in Japan – sent word that the conditions imposed on his kebab van made it impossible to go ahead – though one suspects the backlash was also a factor.

"I cannot, as a small business operator, afford these very stringent conditions," Esen said. "Anyone who actually understood the recommendation and the conditions imposed could not honestly believe that I had been given favourable consideration.

"I actually think it's the exact opposite. Because of these conditions placed on me by council there is no way that I could operate any sort of viable business on this site."

Keira Street

A sad reunion

It had shaped up to be a good night for the three Stafford brothers, who had not been together for two years. A night of laughter, memories and a few beers at the Illawarra Hotel. It wasn't supposed to end in tragedy on the footpath outside.

The youngest brother David met his eldest sibling, 43-year-old Thomas, at the hotel at 10am one Thursday in April, 1953. They'd gotten a very big head-start on middle brother Edward, who couldn't make it until 3.30pm - presumably he was the only one who had to work that day.

The siblings stayed at the Illawarra Hotel for another few hours, leaving the hotel and ending up in Keira Lane, before deciding they should catch a taxi and then headed to the rank on Keira Street.

On the walk, Thomas slipped on the edge of the gutter in Keira Street and staggered backwards to try and regain his balance. Momentum worked against him and Thomas hit his head on a wall and then the footpath.

Thomas would spend about a week in hospital before dying of the injuries on April 11.

"It all happened so quickly," David told the coroner of the tragic moment. "One minute he was standing and the next he was on the footpath unconscious."

Despite having been at a pub for eight hours before the tragic moment, David insisted they hadn't had too much to drink. "We were not drunk, but pretty merry, [Thomas] a little more so than the rest of us."

But it didn't quite look that way to others. Francis Gambrill had been parked in his car outside the hotel, waiting for a friend, when he saw the brothers walking along the road. To him it looked like they were arguing amongst themselves in the moments before Thomas fell, though he said he did not see any punches thrown.

The police said there were no suspicious circumstances and the coroner ruled the death had been caused by an accident.

Frank Best

Frank Best had been struggling ever since he returned from Antarctica in 1931. A soldier wounded during The Somme in World War I, Best had been a seaman on Sir Douglas Mawson's expedition to the coldest continent in 1930-31. But readjusting to life on the land wasn't easy - though he felt alcohol helped. In October 1932, the 39-year-old Best was in court for creating a disturbance at the Melbourne offices of the Sons of Temperance.

Group secretary HR Francis said he had helped Best on a number of occasions after his return from the Antarctic. "He was often very despondent and he sometimes threatened to take poison or to drown himself," a court report stated.

Rather than sentence him, the court gave him a week to find a job on a ship. So he and the Salvation Army's Colonel Bray were regularly down at the Melbourne docks trying to find someone to take him on. Whether they were successful is unclear; Best disappears from the media reports for a few years from this point.

He pops up again in June 1934 amid reports of the King's desire to personally award Polar Medals to all of Mawson's crew at Buckingham Palace. Heartbreakingly for Best, no-one could find him. His mother in England hadn't heard from him for three years, though she believed he was in Australia.

Despite Australian newspapers reporting on the hunt for the missing medal-winner, the Buckingham Palace ceremony went on without him. He was found a month later at the Melbourne City Mission; not believing he was to receive a medal until someone showed him a newspaper. Whether he ever got that medal is unclear.

He played his part in the story of Keira Street in December 1937, when he smashed a window on the strip. After his arrest, Best appeared in court wearing a shirt, tattered pants and no boots; he had shredded his own clothes while in the police cells. Best said he was drunk at 11am when he went to where his wife was working at Dr Raymond Holmes' house at 100 Keira Street, asking to see her.

"I wanted to see my wife and the people in the house treated me like an arrogant child and told me to run away," Best said by way of explaining why he put his fist through a window.

"I admit I did not go the right way about things. I was a member of Mawson's expedition to the South Pole and had to pass a special medical examination to go with the expedition and look at me now."

The court fined him for drunkenness and for the window smashing, but also looked to send him to Long

Keira Street

Bay jail, where the judge thought his drinking could be treated.

"You appear to be a man of determination," the judge told him. "If you make up your mind to leave the drink alone, you ought to be able to do so."

"I admit your worship has been reasonable with me," Best replied. "The drink had got me. It has got me naked – almost

"Drink had beaten me. It has taken my wife and home from me. It has beaten me. It is time I tried to beat it."

And it's possible he did - from that point on there are no more court reports about Frank Best.

Stop light

If you think traffic along Keira Street is a bit rough now, imagine what it might be like without any traffic lights. Because that's what it was like until the mid-1950s, even at the key intersection with Crown Street. Back then, there was no mall so it was a four-way intersection with a traffic cop in the centre during peak periods. How traffic moved through there at other times of the day is a bit of a mystery.

Part of the increase in traffic congestion was because Keira Street had become the city's second most important commercial strip, after sections of Crown street. Another reason was a war between rival bus companies.

In 1948 it seemed the drivers of various bus companies who had a route that took them west along Crown Street and right into Keira tended to dawdle along Keira Street. The *Mercury* reported some buses were leaving the intersection around seven minutes later than the posted time on the timetable; they should have been in and out in just three minutes.

The reason for the go slow was that the drivers were hoping to loiter around Keira and Crown in the hope of snaffling some of their rivals' passengers. Police Inspector Hill told the council he had noticed a conga line of seven or eight buses moving along Crown and into Keira.

"When the leading vehicle arrives at the bus stop," Insp Hill said, " those following are forced to stop in the centre of the roadway until the first vehicle picks up passengers, and a similar procedure is adopted by the following buses.

"This approach also causes the passengers to approach and enter buses in the roadway, thus creating a danger to themselves and other road users."

Several solutions to put an end to the bus war were floated. One put forward by the council's traffic inspector was an "official starter". Someone would have to wait at the Crown and Keira stop to flag a bus in and then wave the flag to dismiss them as per the timetable. As jobs go, it seemed pretty boring. Bus proprietors agreed with that idea, rather than perhaps telling their own drivers to stop the slow cruising in the first place.

A more sensible option was to re-route some of the buses so they all weren't using Crown Street; get some of them travelling along Burelli Street instead. Though some aldermen were concerned about buses stopping at Burelli and Keira, then having to make the climb up to the Crown Street intersection. The bus union didn't want to see the route change either, because they felt sorry for the impact on the poor housewife running errands in the city and having to walk a whole block further to the bus stop.

"One would not expect a housewife to walk from Burelli Street into Crown Street after she had left the bus to do her shopping," a bus union spokesman said, "or to return to Burelli Street from Crown Street, laden with parcels to catch a bus."

Perhaps the best solution was traffic lights, and in 1949 a group of Wollongong traders (uninspiringly called Wollongong Traders) began agitating for them. Keira and Crown was the obvious choice, but they also wanted to see them at the Smith Street and Burelli Street intersections. And also at the Crown Street intersections of Denison and Corrimal streets. Obviously no-one warned them about not being greedy by asking for too much.

Showing that bureaucracy has always moved slowly, it wasn't until 1953 when the issue had gained some momentum – though only for the Keira-Crown street lights. There was a most unusual hiccup – a fruit barrow. Seems a Mr Walker would park his barrow on Keira Street close to the intersection and the council had to debate how to get him to move it, because no parking was to be allowed 90 metres from the proposed lights.

Some wanted to play nice and politely ask Mr Walker to move. Others said bugger that, Walker was breaking the law. Seems you could sell fruit from a barrow only if you didn't also have a store. Walker had also been selling fruits and veggies from a Crown Street shopfront.

Keira Street

The fruit barrow was obviously moved for on December 1, 1955, Mayor JJ Kelly switched on the city's first traffic lights at Keira and Crown (in case you've ever wondered, the JJ stood for Jeremiah Joseph).

"More than 50 years ago we used to have a gas lamplighter on his rounds every night," Mayor JJ said of the council-installed lights. "Then came the electric light 30 years ago. It was opposed but we must have progress."

But if they solved the congestion in town, no-one was going to oppose those traffic lights.

A train line through suburbia

In the early decades of the 20th century, if you stood at the intersection of Keira and Smith Street and looked north, you'd eventually see a train crossing Flinders Street (underneath the road) and heading to the beach. It would be pulling carts full of coal down from the mines in the hills.

There is the tiniest remnant of it still visible down in Osbourne Park opposite Belmore Basin but the rest of it is long gone. But the effect it had on the layout of the city can be seen to this day.

Aerial photos of the city from 1938 show its route. It ran along the main rail line, until a spur bent eastward near where the Throsby Drive overpass is now. From there it curled around the southern edge of what is now Collegians and then travelled to the harbour in between Campbell and Smith streets. It travelled right through what is now the Builders' car park on Church Street, running along the southern edge.

That 1938 aerial shot also shows what appear to be

Keira Street

coal cars taking the curve behind the modern-day Collegians.

By 1940 coal was being shipped out via Port Kembla meaning that the tramway was no longer required and so the railway tracks were taken up. But the scar the rail line left was still visible for decades afterwards.

In the years after the closure, there was debate about what should happen to this corridor that ran west to east through the city. In 1941, after three years of negotiation with the railways, the city council decided to buy the land.

There was talk of turning it into a road, even though there were already several streets heading in exactly that direction. In 1946, the NSW Housing Department said, if the council did build the road, it would consider acquiring the land on either side for housing. The council decided against that idea, but could be swayed if the government agreed to cough up half the cost of the road.

In truth, the council didn't seem to know what to do with the corridor. Later in 1946 they were considering using it for housing but then a year later, the idea of turning it into a road was back on the agenda.

That was made clear in a 1949 *Mercury* story that reported a letter being sent to state Housing Minister Clive Evatt suggesting the corridor could be used to build homes for "elderly people". Evatt implied to the paper that the council "had not yet formulated its policy in reference to the Mt Keira Tramway".

Even though they'd had at least a decade to work it out.

By the mid-1950s, the Education department was

talking up plans to build the road itself – at least a section between Church and Kembla streets – so as to offer rear access to a school on the northern side of Smith Street. Whatever the council planned for the corridor, it wasn't that – they nixed the idea.

Looking at aerial images of the city over the following years, it seems the council took ages to work out what to do. The photos from the air show the steady growth of the city, as suburbia becomes ever more dense. And yet, the scar of the rail corridor is still clearly visible; houses built with Smith and Campbell street frontages could peer over the back fence at this strange no-man's land where nothing seemed destined to be built.

It wasn't until the early 1970s – more than 30 years after the tram line ceased carrying coal – that buildings started to appear along the corridor. Because it was this long skinny space in the middle of the city, it was effectively only long, skinny apartment blocks that could be built there. So they would be built on an east-west alignment, with only one end having street access, while the surrounding suburban blocks were facing north-south.

And so it remains to this day. Those long apartment blocks – such as 35 Kembla Street, 54 Church Street and at 76 and 91 Corrimal Street – serve as a reminder of the route those coal deliveries travelled.

On a modern-day aerial map you can follow the line of those skinny apartment blocks and see where the rail tracks once were. Incidentally, the long-extinct rail line also explains another oddity of the cityscape – the reason why the southern edge of Collegians has that curved shape rather than the boundary line being taken straight to the edge of Flinders Street.

That's where the rail spur came out and crossed Flinders Street. So the block that Collegians now occupies was shaped decades before the leagues club arrived there.

Trouble with tyres

When it comes to legal defences "I bought them off a man in the street" isn't one of the best. But it's the one Tom Dion opted for during a May 1931 court appearance after he was charged with buying stolen tyres.

The cops visited Dion's Fairy Meadow home, following up on claims his bus was sporting hot tyres. When a Detective Constable by the name of McCarthy asked for an explanation as to where he got those tyres, Dion replied "I bought them off a man in the street at Wollongong last Wednesday". He couldn't produce a cheque stub because he paid in cash and, unusual for a businessman, Dion said he'd forgotten to ask for a receipt.

Dion told the detective he'd never seen the man before in his life. The guy had just jumped on the bus at Crown Street and asked Tom if he could do with some tyres – they'd cost £10 each. Tom was all good with that, though he'd have to go home and get the money first.

On his return, he found the man in Keira Street and

bought the tyres. It doesn't appear the mystery man was carrying the tyres around the city streets; a witness who claimed to see the transaction said the man had pulled the tyres from a car he'd parked nearby.

The police detective still wasn't buying Dion's story. To him, it all seemed too good to be true; the police had recently seized two of his buses (the court reports do not say why) and here was Dion having just picked up a replacement bus and was in urgent need of new tyres for it. McCarthy put it to Dion that it seemed an interesting coincidence.

"Yes, it does seem funny," Dion replied.

The detective also noted it was curious that identifying numbers and other markings had been removed from both tyres; they had been rubbed off one of the tyres and someone appeared to go at the other with a knife.

Though in court, McCarthy said his enquiries led him to conclude Dion had a reputation as a man of good character and admitted that sometimes peculiar coincidences that may point to guilt turn out to have innocent meanings.

In this case, what got Dion off the hook was his claim that what he bought were "job tyres"; second grade tyres the makers don't want to sell under their own name. So they remove their own markings. Also helping the case was a Bulli mechanic who testified a man claiming to be from the Goodyear company had been there a few weeks earlier, trying to flog some "job tyres".

The magistrate dismissed the charges – drawing a cheer from the gallery – but told Dion that if this was the way he had been operating, then he wasn't showing the best business sense.

Keira Street

The Mall

One of the biggest changes along Keira Street happened at the Crown Street intersection. We're talking about the creation of the mall in 1985. It took years to get to that point and, ever since it was finished, people have been insisting it should be ripped out and reopened to traffic.

It now seems a thoroughly moot point that the mall is here to stay. Reopening the road to cars would mean knocking down that pedestrian bridge – and the restaurant set up inside it – linking the two halves of Wollongong Central. It would also mean reversing all the work that went into making lower Crown Street immediately east of the mall a one-way street. Having two-way traffic travelling along Crown Street only to hit a headache at Kembla Street is problem best avoided. Don't people remember the pain caused by not being able to drive through the Keira Street transit mall?

The idea of shutting down a section of Crown Street was being spoken about for years before the mall actually happened. Back in May 1969, the *Mercury* floated the idea of a car-free Crown Street. "Conversion of Crown Street, Wollongong, into a traffic-free shopping mall would sharply lift city retail sales, according to experts," the paper reported. "It would give Wollongong a tourist attraction which would create worldwide interest."

The paper was clearly gilding the lily with the whole "worldwide interest" thing. And as for those "experts", there was only one mentioned in the story and he only spoke generally about the effect of malls and never spoke directly about one in Wollongong. Those who did – from the chamber of commerce, city town planners and aldermen – weren't in favour.

Still, the talk of a mall didn't go away. A year later the *Mercury* reported on the city council planning to close the strip from Keira to Kembla. As part of the plan, there would be a ring of eight parking stations built, each capable of holding 500 cars. The first, in Keira Street south of Burelli, was already under construction.

"Alderman Clark said other parking stations might be built in Atchison Street, MacCabe Park, Corrimal Street, Victoria Street, Kembla Street, Church Street and Keira Street," the *Mercury* reported.

Alderman Clark was quite a booster for the mall concept, keeping the idea on the radar. "The mall is definitely something that must come," he said. "It would be a traffic-free shopping plaza with shrubs and trees.

Keira Street

"Of course the traffic flow would have to be revised, and we would have a problem with the buses but this should not be too difficult to overcome."

But it seemed it was too difficult to overcome because, by 1975, there was still no mall. At least not a permanent one. In December of that year, the council had made plans for a 12 Days of Christmas festival, which would see Crown Street between Keira and Kembla closed from December 8 to January 5 – which the council mustn't have realised was clearly longer than 12 days.

The festival plans hit a stumbling block when NSW Police Commissioner Fred Hanson refused permission for the road closure – despite a similar closure happening for a Christmas event a year earlier. Alderman and festival organiser R Hall called the letter announcing the refusal "the most narrow and short-minded letter Wollongong council has ever received".

"The commissioner should open his eyes to what Wollongong wants and not what the police department wants," Alderman Hall said.

A compromise was reached a day later which would see the stretch of Crown Street closed for two Thursday late night shopping nights – December 11 and 18. After that first night, Lord Mayor Frank Arkell – who had been championing the mall – declared it a success. "You could feel the excitement swelling up in people," Lord Mayor Arkell said shortly before the barriers were removed at 9pm. "No-one knocked it; everyone enjoyed it."

It was back a year later but stayed in place way after the Christmas period. In February Arkell used his casting vote to break a deadlock and see the closure continue for another two months. The reason was to analyse the traffic effects of a longer closure. The barricades came down in April 1977 but it would be another eight years before work began on a permanent structure.

In 1984, the council's plans to build the mall got what is now called an anchor tenant when Grace Bros agreed to take up a key spot in the soon-to-be constructed Gateway Centre. "Today is a champagne day for the wonderful city of Wollongong," Arkell said. "I am delighted that our planning has been rewarded by attracting Australia's premier retailer, Grace Bros."

Part of the enthusiasm for the mall had been driven by the economic slump the city had been suffering through in the early 1980s. Getting the approval of Grace Bros was seen as a marker that the city was moving onto better times – not unlike the more recent decision of GPT to build Wollongong Central.

On Sunday, August 11, 1985, there was a festival atmosphere as Arkell formally closed the street ahead of construction. A fleet of buses were among the last vehicles to travel down Crown Street. In the early stages of construction the section between Church and Kembla streets would be used as a car park, with kerbside and angled parking spaces marked out.

A front page story in the *Mercury* the following day included a detailed description of how people could get around the city.

"East of the mall, both Kembla and Corrimal streets will provide a direct route north and south of the city centre. West of the mall, alternate routes will be available via Market, Young, Governors Lane, Railway Parade or Victoria, Hercules and New Dapto Roads.

"Vehicles travelling east and west, north of the mall should use either Smith or Market streets. Burelli Street also provides a direct route near the city centre as well as providing access to roads for destinations north and south of the city."

It is interesting that no mention is made of Atchison Street, the road many people coming into town along Crown Street use to get around the mall.

The big day came on October 20, 1986, and was deemed so important to the city that *Mercury* published a 100-page supplement tagged A City Reborn. In it Lord Mayor Arkell said "after three years of serious economic difficulties, Wollongong has turned adversity into prosperity".

"The mall is beyond description … it is glorious and it means Wollongong is now a city of the 21st century."

That liftout also included an interview with the mall's architect Tony Corkill, who admitted he was aiming to create a bit of controversy. "Even if it is not widely accepted by everyone, as long as it projects a strong image it will be an important feature in the city," Corkill said.

He also tackled the feature of the mall that would attract criticism for as long as it was there – the birdcage. "There is nothing wrong with it looking like a birdcage as long as it is big enough," he said. "Some of the most beautiful structures in the world house birds. There used to be a steel structure in the Botanic Gardens [in Sydney] for birds it is was a great piece of architecture."

The Wollongong Mall was officially opened by the Premier Barrie Unsworth, who unveiled a plaque on the amphitheatre at the centre of the mall. "What you did as a community was to work together – all elements, management, labour, local government – you all worked together," Unsworth said. "What we are seeing here is the start of a great new future for Wollongong and the Illawarra."

The mall and the new Gateway Centre also were a great opportunity for shoplifters too. Police Sergeant Frank Grogan was expecting shoplifting gangs to target the new shopping strip. "I've no doubt they will come from far and wide to take advantage of the crowded shops," he said. "Many of the professionals are adept at identifying shop floorwalkers and the police presence should help."

The mall would go on to have its detractors, and the call to rip it up and re-open it to traffic would keep coming up over the years. The closest the city got to tearing it up was in late 2006, when the council preferred to re-open the mall to one-way traffic at night, subject to designs and costings reports. However, the ICAC corruption scandal kicked off in 2008, which put paid to those plans as the council was placed in the hands of administrators.

Those administrators scrapped the council's decision and in April 2009 decided to keep it pedestrian-only but carry out a $17.8 million upgrade. That upgrade included the removal of the birdcage.

Something else had already been torn down by that time. In 2000, the pink wall at the Keira St entrance was knocked down to allow for the pedestrian walkway to connect the Gateway and Crown Central – which were both owned by Lend Lease. Part of the objection was that the wall presented as a barrier between eastern and western Crown Street, but Lord Mayor David Campbell said it would be "foolish" to keep it and allow the walkway to be built just two metres away. But that walkway didn't have total support on the council.

"This isn't a pedestrian walkway, it's a shopping complex," Cr Pat Franks said. "It will be the death knell of the mall."

It was a prediction that proved to be very wrong – more than 20 years later, the mall is still there. Though there is little doubt the idea of re-opening it to traffic will still be voiced for years to come.

The street lights up

These days it's hard to find any dark corners along Keira Street, not even at the footpath that lies underneath the overhang from what was once known as the Crown Gateway Centre. Sure, that section is always in shade during the day but lighting underneath brightens things up at night.

It can be hard to imagine there was a time when it might have been tricky to negotiate the street at night with perhaps little aside from the glow of the moon and stars to help you on your way. But there was a time that happened, so it was a big deal when the city's first gas-lit street lamp was switched on – located on the corner of Keira and Smith streets – way back on August 20, 1883.

It was a moment that was almost two years in the making. In May 1881, a public meeting was held to push for a gasworks for Wollongong. Ahead of that, the committee had gone from house to house, business to business to gauge whether there was enough interest in better lighting than that which came from a candle. They found there was certainly enough to interest someone coming in to set up a gasworks.

"We see strong reasons for believing that a company to supply gas to the town of Wollongong is a perfectly safe commercial undertaking that will pay good and highly satisfactory profits to shareholders of such company," the committee's report stated.

Work finally started in November 1882 when engineer John Davies came to town. The plan was to build the gasworks in Charlotte Street, but Davies' first job was to lay the gas mains along the city streets. The mains went up Flinders Street and along Keira Street to the Crown Street intersection.

From there they headed east to Corrimal Street, past the market square on the corner of Market and Harbour and ending at the Brighton Hotel near Belmore Basin.

"Mr Davies considers the site chosen for the gasworks is of the best he has ever seen," the *Mercury* reported, "and expects to have the town lighted with gas within a few months hence."

"A few months hence" actually turned out to actually be 10 months, and there was a bit of a celebration when that first lamp on the corner of Keira and Smith was lit up.

At 5pm on August 20, 1883, the city's aldermen visited the gasworks, where they were shown all the equipment, "the visit thus rendered all the more interesting," the *Mercury* said, no doubt exaggerating things quite a lot. Then they headed over to the manager's residence, drank some champagne and then went to the corner of Keira and Smith streets where chairman of the board, a Captain Owen, did the honours with the first public gas lamp.

"The town, or rather the parts of it within the range of gas mains, presented quite a novel and improved night appearance," the *Mercury* said. "The effects of gaslight in some instances was particularly striking."

After that, they adjourned to the Freemasons Hotel, on the northwestern corner of Keira and Crown, for even more champagne – because turning on a light switch is very thirsty work. There Mr Davies gave himself a pat on the back, ensuring the locals that the Wollongong gasworks "were not surpassed for perfection by any other gasworks in the colony". Sure, the Sydney gasworks were bigger, he said, but not better.

The celebrations wrapped up at 11pm and everyone went home full of champagne, along roads that were now so much brighter at night.

Keira Street

Tuning in

For decades, one commercial radio station had Wollongong all to itself. The station 2WL kicked off way back in July 1931; and if you wanted to listen to local radio that was all you had – for more than 40 years. For some reason it wasn't until the mid-1970s that the federal government decided a second station would be a good idea, so it launched a call for groups interested in acquiring the second licence.

The controversial winner announced in January 1978 was Wollongong City Radio. They were controversial because of concerns about trade unions' involvement in the group. The NSW Trades and Labour Council was the group's single-biggest shareholder with 42,000 shares – 6 per cent of the total. On top of that, six unions each held 2 per cent of the shares. To some that made it highly probable that the unions would take over the radio station – a concern that had been raised by a rival bidder for the licence.

"I think it is quite likely some of the prospective shareholders in Wollongong City Radio – because of changed economic times – may find it preferable not to find the necessary capital of $1 million to $1.5 million to set up the station," a spokesman for the rival said. "This could lead to greater trade union control over the station."

To counteract that, Wollongong City Radio said no one shareholder could own more than 14 per cent and any transfer of shares would be monitored so as to maintain the original shareholding breakdown.

The plan was for the new station to cater to the kids, with a top 40 format. "We hope to have young people running the station," said WCR chairman Ralph Hopkins, "and they will decide what is played."

After a few months, the name of the station came out – it was 2OO. Which always seemed an odd choice because those two letter Os, can easily look like zeroes.

How does this radio station fit into the story of Keira Street? Well, they managed to have a spare $250,000 to buy the Grand Hotel on the corner of Keira and Burelli. The early plan was to carry out some renovations to the ground floor at the Burelli Street entrance to turn it into a studio, while still allowing the pub and accommodation side of things to carry on (though the station would end up broadcasting from the first floor). It would turn around and lease out the pub to a third party, thereby making a tidy return on its investment even before a single record was played.

Keira Street

The radio station was serious in other ways too – they had managed to lure Rod Muir down from Sydney's 2SM, where he'd sent that station's ratings soaring.

The new station began broadcasting at 12.01am on January 1, 1978, and also organised a concert across the road at MacCabe Park featuring Jon English and Doug Parkinson. But the idea of a studio inside a pub didn't sit well with the licencing police. They had won a case that stopped 2OO from removing the licence from the first floor of The Grand, raising concerns about how communication between licenced and de-licenced parts of the hotel would take place.

But the station won an appeal, Judge Gee saying he didn't think guests and drinkers at the Grand would interfere with the studio operations.

That wasn't an end to the stations troubles with operating out of a pub. In May 1979, 2OO was fined $300 for breaching the Liquor Act after carrying out renovations to the hotel without the consent of the Licencing Court. A few months later in October, they ran afoul of the Licencing Court again. This time it was because of conditions requested by Judge Gee back in April – including a unisex toilet on the first floor and a better approach to access for after-hours hotel guests – had not been fulfilled. The station manager said a builder had been employed on that very day to take care of the renovations.

By the way, if you don't recognise either 2WL or 2OO, that's because they don't exist in that format any more.

Both moved over to the FM band in 1992 to become WAVE FM and i98fm respectively.

A Keira Street shooting

In the early years of the 1900s, Keira Street was a place for young men to hang out on the corner, doing heinous things like, umm, not stepping aside whenever some upstanding member of the public wanted to pass by. It so outraged a Magistrate by the name of Gates that he used his courtroom to voice his feelings on this abhorrent practice.

"If the parents could not keep their children off the streets," the *Mercury* of June 12, 1914 reported of Gates' tirade, "he recommended the police to bring them up before him and he would have them sent away to a reformatory."

Locked up for not getting out of someone's way? Sounds a bit harsh, if you ask me.

"They loitered at the corners and showed no inclination to get out of the way of passersby. He had only been in the streets of Wollongong a few nights and this was one of the things that impressed itself on him," the *Mercury* continued. "The loafers would not get out of his way and he did not know how the ladies fared."

What was particularly odd about Magistrate Gates' rant – aside from the pomposity that the lower classes shouldn't impede his progress – was that it came at the end of a court case about a very serious incident.

A shooting on Keira Street. Yep, someone shot someone else and the guy with the gavel was banging on about boys hanging out on the corner. The shooting occurred on Sunday, May 11, 1914, outside Jarman's Grocer ("the store where quality counts"). Working out where Jarman had his shop – or where most shops were around this time – can be tricky. In their newspaper ads, businesses didn't bother with putting a street number, just the street. So BJ Benham was in Auburn Street, FO Wiseman in Crown Street and Jarman's in Keira Street. If you were lucky the ad would state it was next to some other business – which is only really helpful if you knew where that other business was. One imagines the locals wandering along the street, looking around at random for the grocer, the draper or the mechanic. Perhaps the CBD in the early 1910s was small enough that you could walk it in a minute or two.

Jarman's place was previously known as the Beehive (why, I don't have a clue) and a photo shows that store right next to the Salvation Army Citadel on the southwestern corner of Keira and Victoria streets. By the way, calling the place a "citadel" makes it seem more grandiose than it really was. Photos show a bland brick rectangle with a window on either side of the front door. Imagine a five-year-old's drawing of a house and you're

Keira Street

pretty much on the money.

Anyway, back to the story of the shooting. Our gunman was Ernest Strong, aged 16 years (and two months, the *Mercury* reported, as though those extra 60 days made any difference). A very small boy for his age, the reports stated, Strong was walking north along Keira Street, towards the Smith Street intersection. With him were siblings Violet and Reg Davison. They had met up earlier in the evening and had showed them his revolver. Somewhere in town – the court reports don't say where – Strong fired the seven-shot revolver five times, Reg once, leaving a single bullet in the chamber.

As the trio neared the Victoria Street corner, they came across a gang of teens – the type the magistrate was so worried about. When Violet and Reg passed them earlier in the evening, Strong said he heard one of them call the red-headed Violet "ginger". So on the second meeting he decided to confront the alleged insulter – a 14-year-old named James Hickey. He offered to fight Strong, who must have been agreeable as he suggested they head over to a paddock and duke it out.

Showing a sudden lack of bravado, Hickey backed off and headed back to his gang. The trio followed and Strong heard Hickey say "here's my mob now – what are you going to do?". Reg Davison later said Strong told them he would take them on one at a time but if he came at them all at once he would shoot.

He then stuck his hand into his left coat pocket, where he held the revolver. While issuing the threat, unbeknown to Strong, gang member Fred Walker had managed to get around behind him. He grabbed Strong's arms, there was a struggle, and the gun - carrying just that single bullet – went off.

The bullet entered Walker's right side, just below his chest and close to the spinal column; for that reason the piece of metal was left in situ rather than risk it being removed.

Strong later admitted in court that he'd bought the gun for protection after being attacked a week earlier by three older boys who said they were going to wait for him on Keira Street. Magistrate Gates was shocked someone had sold a gun "to a boy who did not look more than 12 or 13", saying they should be "downright ashamed of themselves".

Strong also insisted that he pulled the trigger of the gun – which was still in his pocket – as a warning. "The boy that was holding me was a bigger boy than I am," Strong told police. "I was a stranger and didn't know anybody. I was frightened they would give me a thrashing.

"The revolver was in my left coat pocket. I put my hand in and fired it off. I did not know he was shot until afterwards."

An inspection of the coat backed up Strong's story; there was a bullet hole near the pocket of his coat.

Walker testified that he had recovered from the wounding. He also insisted he was not the ringleader of any gang. "We meet and go to the pictures together or play football together," he told the court.

Magistrate Gates felt no good would be served by taking the case further and so dismissed any charges

Keira Street

against Strong. He also warned that if the police saw any of the gang loitering in Keira Street again they were to be brought before the court and he would see that they were sent to a reformatory.

Murder!

Located on Keira Street since 1973, Amigos lays claim to being the longest continually operating Mexican restaurant in Australia. That could possibly be true though it's hard to see how one could prove that. It's unlikely anyone had been keeping tabs on the rise and fall of the country's Mexican joints.

Something else the restaurant lays claim to is being the home of an infamous murder, even once including that information on their menus. Though that may or may not be entirely true. Yes, there was a murder upstairs, at 118 Keira Street, but Amigos is at 116 Keira Street. No118 is nothing but a door onto the street. Granted it is entirely possible some renovations went on since the 1971 murder that changed the street numbering. Wouldn't be the first time on Keira Street; it appears that as the street got longer the numbers on the properties changed, which understandably made it tricky to research this book.

Various owners are convinced someone came to grief upstairs – because they've got the ghost stories to prove it. Former co-owner Deb Langton said she'd seen become quite familiar with the ghost the staff had named Charlie. The aircon and microwaves have turned themselves on, bottles on shelves have moved and she's heard someone say 'hello' only to look up and find no-one there.

"Staff have seen someone walk down the stairs and out of the building without anyone being here," Langton said. "My son, when he was two, went up the stairs and was screaming his head off saying 'a pirate came out of the wall!'. Another guy went upstairs and said he saw a man leaning against the mantelpiece and when he turned back he was gone."

But it seems Charlie listens when you want him to give the tomfoolery a rest. Langton and a friend were painting in the restaurant one day and the music volume – the control was upstairs – kept going up and down.

"My friend yelled upstairs 'can you just stop playing around with the music, you're really starting to fucking piss me off' and it stopped happening."

Back in 1971, the business at 118 Keira Street was called the Tiki Coffee Lounge. While the place did sell coffee, it wasn't all they sold. It was really a brothel, with the waitresses doubling as prostitutes. A customer could take their pick of the ladies, pay $10 and go to one of the two bedrooms upstairs. The women put the $10 in the till and took a ticket from a docket book; at the end of the day those tickets would be counted up and they'd be paid $5 per stub.

There was a buzzer system installed where a single

buzz would call a heavy upstairs to sort out a troublesome client while two buzzes meant the woman wanted more time.

A Sydney police officer later told a court hearing that a suspect had named businessman Anthony Malouf as the owner of the Tiki club. The same court heard the other owner was a Wollongong police sergeant, which goes some way to explaining how a brothel could operate so close to the police station.

The ghost named 'Charlie' was Charles Berry, who ran the Tiki club – at least until he disappeared in January 1971. In May, before Berry's body was even found, police charged Michael Hannigan with his murder, claiming he hit Berry with a hammer and then shot him twice. Berry's body was later discovered in a shallow grave at Bendalong near Nowra on June 16.

Hannigan wasn't the only one charged over Berry's murder. Also facing a murder charge was Malouf (though he would be discharged after the committal hearing). Another man, Peter Soffe (who had to be extradited from New Zealand for the trial), was charged over harbouring Hannigan after the murder while soldier Ian Adrian Williamson faced counts relating to the disposal of Berry's body.

The court heard McHannigan hadn't exactly kept quiet about the murder. Detective Sergeant ER Day from Sydney's CIB said McHannigan had spilled the beans about the whole thing. Sgt Day said McHannigan described Malouf as the Mr Big of the Wollongong crime scene.

Keira Street

In Day's record of interview, McHannigan explained the motive for the murder was Malouf's offer of taking over Berry's job. Malouf said, with plans to open a brothel in Port Kembla and another in Jervis Bay, there would be a lot of money for McHannigan.

"Then he [Malouf] said 'we are going to get rid of Charlie because we don't want him to have the business'. He said 'would you like to get rid of him because we are going to do it in any case and if you are not involved, you will probably go too. There is no use going to the police because they won't give you any help'."

When Soffe, who was working as a doorman at the Tiki, arrived at work on the day of the alleged conversation, McHannigan spoke to him about the murder. They decided to do it on the morning of January 6. Day's interview had McHannigan saying that Soffe volunteered to shoot Berry as he slept. But Soffe said the angle wasn't great and told McHannigan to get a hammer and hit him first.

He did that and, after the strike, Berry sat up and McHannigan ran out to turn up the music from a record player to mask the noise of the gunshot.

McHannigan's fiancee Beverley Eames (who worked at the Tiki club but insisted in court it was as a dancer and not a prostitute) also told the court he had confessed everything to her. McHannigan allegedly told her that while Berry's body had been stored in the attic space gases had made it expand. When it came time to remove the body someone – Soffe insisted it was McHannigan himself – had to stomp on it to make it smaller to fit through the hole in the ceiling. While they were doing that, McHannigan told her he was wearing a handkerchief covered in Brut 33 to mask the smell.

Which is where Williamson came in. He told police McHannigan had forced him to help. "I want you to help us get rid of the body," he told police McHannigan had said. "Don't cross me or I will put you in the same position as he is in."

He had parked his car at the rear of the Tiki club, removing the spare tyre and tools from the boot. Then, while the others were bringing down Berry's body, Williamson went for a walk up Keira Street. Twenty minutes later he came back to see them closing the boot of his car. They told him Berry was in there, wrapped in blankets.

Williamson drove to a Cringila service station, got some fly spray and aftershave to deal with the aromatic side effects of Berry's decomposing body, and then drove south.

At Bendalong, he drove into a clearing in the bush and started digging a hole, then taking Berry's body from the boot. It was dreadful work; Williamson said he was sick several times.

Soffe, who had already pleaded guilty to being an accessory after the fact, told police McHannigan had done the killing alone. Soffe claimed McHannigan had turned up the music and then walked up the stairs. A few minutes later he called down to Soffe for some assistance, which is when he went up and found Berry's body lying on the bed.

Keira Street

"Mike [some knew McHannigan as 'Big Mike'] told me he had killed him," Soffe told the police. " He had the gun in his hand and I assumed that he had shot him. He told me later he had hit him with a hammer and pumped a couple of bullets into him."

Soffe added the information that Berry's son was downstairs at the time of the murder, and McHannigan said they had to kill the boy as well.

"I said to Mike 'I want to go downtown'. I wanted to get him away from the kid so nothing would happen to him and I wanted to get out of the place as well. I was shaking and sweating all over and I had a throbbing headache."

In court, McHannigan denied telling Beverley anything. He also claimed he "chickened out" at the last minute, running from the room as Soffe held the gun. "I heard the gun fire as I was going down the stairs," he said from the dock.

"When I was at the bottom I heard another shot. The next time I saw Charles Berry he was dead. I didn't shoot Charles Berry." McHannigan's lawyer noted that was the same story he'd given to the police months earlier.

The jury didn't buy it, finding McHannigan guilty. Justice O'Brien then sentenced him to life in prison.

Wiliamson was also found guilty of being an accessory after the fact. Both he and Soffe were sentenced to eight years. Williamson won a retrial, an appeals court finding it was an error of law that the judge had directed the jury to ignore Williamson's claims of being threatened by McHannigan.

It didn't do him much good. A second trial ended with the same result – eight years jail for Williamson.

Music Farmers

Down at the southern end of Keira Street, underneath that dreaded dark space caused by the old Crown Gateway built out across the road sits a survivor of the Wollongong music scene.

In the age of music streaming services, record stores have been having a rough time. Aside from vinyl collectors, hardly anyone actually seems to want to pay for music these days.

Once upon a time there was almost a dozen music stores within a stone's throw of Keira Street. As of 2024 there is just one – Music Farmers. Back in 2004, if you were placing bets as to which record store in the Wollongong CBD would be the only one left standing today, you probably wouldn't be putting your money on Music Farmers.

Jeb Taylor and Simon Dalla Pozza had opened up a tiny store in 2004, upstairs in Central Chambers in the lower half of the Crown Street Mall. Not the most well-known location; there would still be people today who wouldn't have a clue where that was.

"There was a lot of record stores around at that time," Taylor said. "Redback was still there, Rock Factory was still there. I think Wilson's was there and Sanity still existed."

Today they're all gone, but that small shop with the weird name that started out upstairs in the mall is still going today.

Yes, it's moved a few times – to Crown Lane and then to its current location in Keira Street (at least until the WIN Grand development gets going) – but Music Farmers has always been around since those days of 2004.

Taylor said there wasn't any grand plan to start a record store; initially it was meant to be an office and storage space for his HighBeam Music label and distribution business.

"When we started, a lot of the stock was pretty obscure stuff and local bands," Taylor says. "That was our point of difference then. They [all the other record stores] were all competing with each other at the time. We had a small space that we rented ourselves, whereas they were big retail spaces and had to pay lots of wages and stuff like that."

For Taylor, the secret to Music Farmers' longevity is that they started small and took their time to get bigger.

"I think slow growth is what's kept us here rather than trying to be too ambitious too quickly," he said. "You see a lot of businesses coming to Wollongong and they try and set up really big, really quickly - and they don't last. We wouldn't have lasted if we did that."

Keira Street

By 2007, they decided to get quite a bit bigger – relative to the tiny shop upstairs in the mall – and set up in a cavernous space in Crown Lane (where Kneading Ruby is today). This was where Music Farmers made a real move towards vinyl – they'd mainly been stocking and selling CDs before then. That meant the store was ahead of the vinyl resurgence that would start a few years later.

"It was really starting to come back, though Australia was a little bit slower to catch on," Taylor said. "I remember being in Europe in 2010 and just starting to see that vinyl shops were busy and there were a lot of shops – that was my trigger that this would work again in Australia.

"Record Store Days got really big around 2013 and that gave it another sort of kick on. It was still a bit more underground, but then there was a point when all the really big mainstream records started to sell on vinyl as well."

The move to 5 Crown Lane also saw the addition of a cafe, an art gallery and live shows – it was also the time when Dalla Pozza left and current business partner Nick Irwin came on board.

"We just wanted to be able to run shows and run in-stores – and there were a few other people around at the time looking for space as well to do different projects they were working on," Taylor said of 5 Crown Lane.

"That place just gave us heaps of space, maybe too much. Sometimes we'd think 'what are we going to do with all the space?'."

For three years, that space would be used by local artists and musicians until Wollongong City Council spoiled the fun. The venue had been staging bands without the appropriate licence and, when Taylor found how much that would cost, he figured it wasn't worth it.

So they held a final gig in December 2008 and that was it for the venue. The doors were closed, but Taylor and Irwin were still working inside – using it as an office for the record label and online sales. Taylor said the city was changing, with new venues like Music Farmers, Yours & Owls (which was still a cafe at the time) and the Otis bar starting up.

The way he sees it, that caught council by surprise and it didn't know how to deal with these new venues in a regulatory sense. A few years later, council started to realise the value of what it now tagged as "the night-time economy" and this led to Taylor and Irwin to re-open the doors in 2011.

Of course, the construction noises coming from the Wollongong Central shopping centre across the road made it hard for any complaints about a band's loud music to stack up. But then, after they'd suffered through all that noise from the drilling and construction of the shopping centre, Taylor says the landlords at 5 Crown Lane offered them a new lease "which was four to five times what we were paying before".

Taylor and Irwin said no, and ended up in the Keira Street shop where they are now - and there's still space up the back for bands to play a gig.

"The timing was a bit annoying," Taylor says of the

move, "because we put up with construction for two or three years but in hindsight it's been way better being down here anyway. The shop space just became more of a real shop space."

It's also become a record label – Farmer and The Owl – after teaming up with the Yours and Owls guys in 2014. The idea was to do what both Music Farmers and Yours and Owls had been doing; staying in Wollongong and helping to build a scene rather than opting to move to Sydney or Melbourne. "There are so many good bands in our area so the label so the label is a way for us to help get them some wider national attention," Yours and Owls' Ben Tillman said.

The biggest of those bands they would sign was also the first – a Windang duo called Hockey Dad. They would go on to become the biggest band from Wollongong since Tumbleweed.

Taylor had seen them play a year earlier at Rad bar in front of a small crowd. Despite being a new band with only a handful of gigs under their belt, he was impressed. "They were pretty rough and young but there was something behind the roughness in the songs," he said. "You probably don't see it that early with a lot of bands, where you can look through that rawness and feel there is some potential there."

Hockey Dad released the debut EP *Dreamin'* on the new label, following it up with albums like *Blend Inn* and *Brain Candy*. The latter album was only kept out of the No1 spot on the charts by the surprise release of a new album by Taylor Swift. So you must be doing something right if it takes someone of Swift's stature to block your path.

The label Farmer and the Owl also put out a bunch of re-releases and a singles box set from Tumbleweed, frontman Richie Lewis' solo album and releases by local acts like The Pinheads, Private Wives, Totally Unicorn, Kid Pharoah and Charbel.

The label and the record store based in Keira Street has been in no small part responsible for the resurgence of the Wollongong music scene. And its recognition outside of the city. No more is Wollongong thought of as a place of crappy covers bands or acts that can't pull a crowd in Sydney.

Dogs

In July 1952 there was a manhunt for a particularly heinous criminal – one who had been going around the city poisoning dogs. Keira and Crown streets and the surrounding area was the target, with the *Mercury* reporting the man operated at night, dropping baits laced with strychnine in the street and throwing them over fences.

A W Nissen, the manager of Palings at 102 Keira Street, said he had found three dead dogs at the rear of his shop. "It is frightful to poison dogs," he said. "They are wonderful animals. I cannot see why anyone would want to do a thing like that but apparently he is a maniac."

The *Mercury* also reported that 15 dogs had been found in Richardson Street, a laneway a block west of Keira Street. A pup owned by Stan Harrington of Harrington's Car Park – the old name for a car sales yard – in Keira Street near what is now known as Gilligan's Island found his Alsatian pup lying paralysed at the front door when he arrived for work.

Local vets confirmed they had been seeing an abnormal number of dogs that had been poisoned. Police said they had received reports of poisonings but had not started any investigations. The organs of the dogs would not be sent to the government labs for testing, they said, but owners could carry out private tests and then launch prosecutions.

It appears the police never did carry out an investigation or, if they did, no-one was ever caught for there was no report of it in the newspapers. Nor, sadly was the outbreak in 1952 an isolated incident. A year earlier, a dozen dogs had been poisoned in Fairy Meadow, believed to be after eating baits laced with caustic soda. "If we find who is doing the poisoning we will see that justice is done," one Fairy Meadow resident said.

Mrs T Eddy had lost her kelpie named Blinkie to the criminal and initially thought she had a clue to their identity. Three days before Blinkie's death, she got a letter bearing a Wollongong postmark. "Although I am fond of animals," the letter read, "I feel it is time to object to the howling of your dog at all hours of the night. If you do not see clear to stop him I will take the matter and inform Sgt Shaw."

At first she thought it was a note written by the poisoner's own hand, but soon changed her mind. "The note was obviously written by one of my neighbours but I should not like to think any of them would poison my dog," she said. "We think that the dog picked up the bait in the street and it was just a chain of circumstances."

Keira Street

Again, no-one appears to have been arrested for the Fairy Meadow poisonings.

Taking a punt

It's possible Monty Sheppard's chances in the 1932 state election weren't exactly helped by his involvement in a family gambling den. In the late 1920s and early 1930s, Sheppard and brother William ran Sheppard's Billiard Saloon on Keira Street, near the Victoria Street intersection. The police better knew it as a front for gambling, judging by the number of times they raided the place.

In 1932, Monty decided to run for the state seat of Illawarra hoping to unseat incumbent Labor MP Joseph Davies. To confuse matters, Monty also ran as a Labor candidate - but under a "Federal Labor" ticket. Though in his policy speech, he said he represented "sane Labor, not Red Labor".

However, some of his policies didn't seem all that sane, such as the abolition of state governments; yep, he wanted to get rid of the very position he was running for. "One central government for the whole of Australia," he said in his policy speech, "one 44-hour week over the whole of Australia. We want to make Australia a nation not a thing of wrangling, warring states, trying to best the other, likeable to seven families living in the one big house."

His other policies were doubling the dole but making people work for it, a rent reduction for government housing and the cancellation of all war debts.

Those policies didn't grab the electorate – either that or the voters knew his background. Monty came second-last with 201 votes or just 1.36 per cent. Lucky he seemed to have the gambling den to fall back on.

The police had a running battle with the Sheppard brothers' billiard hall. The siblings regularly appeared in court facing charges of SP betting at the saloon. In April 1929, the court heard an outline of how the betting system operated. William would take the bets in the saloon and then get on the phone to Monty, who lived across the road, to keep a tally. The police obviously knew that was how things worked, because they raided both the saloon and Monty's house at the same time.

In that case both brothers pleaded guilty, with the police requesting a small fine as they did not go outside to take bets, nor did they bet with women or children.

Just two months later William was back in court for taking bets at the saloon. His lawyer noted he had only the one conviction "but now had seen the error of his ways and convinced the [police] Inspector that there was nothing further to be feared". The inspector agreed, telling the court he understood that gambling was no longer taking place at Sheppard's Billiard Saloon.

The judge must have believed it as well for he just issued William with a fine. "I am prepared to give you a chance to reform in earnest," the judge said, "but if you come up again it will mean the maximum penalty. I hope the reform was not just for while this case was on."

The brothers may actually have stopped betting, for there were no news reports of them appearing in court for several years. Or maybe they had gotten better at hiding it. At least until 1933, which was when William was back in court on betting charges.

In the interim their billiard hall had been renamed the Wollongong Sports Club and people had to be members to get in. People walked through the front door on the street, where they were greeted by a doorman in front of a second sign reading "Members Only – Show Cards".

In that 1933 raid the police tried the front door, found it locked and then went around to the rear, where another door was also locked. Making their way back to the street entrance, they found it unlocked and walked in brandishing a warrant.

"There were about 100 persons in the room upstairs and about 50 in the room downstairs," a police detective testified. "There was a wireless set in the room upstairs broadcasting races."

A Constable Mannes also gave evidence that, before the detectives raided the club, he had seen William at a table with a pad and pencil, writing down bets from the crowd of men surrounding him. When he saw the detectives bring William into the police station he told them what he'd seen that day.

William took issue with the constable's evidence, claiming it was all made up. The constable, William said, wouldn't have been able to get in. "I am the manager of the club," he told the court. "The front door has never been left open since the premises has been a club and he could not get past the doorkeeper." Also, he said he had not seen Constable Mannes that day until he was brought to the police station.

The judge sided with the police testimony, figuring there was no reason to doubt it and fined William. "A raid was no doubt arranged," the *Mercury*'s report said, "and when the police got there they evidently were delayed for a sufficient time to enable evidence of gambling being got away with."

As well as gambling, the police would regularly haul the billiard saloon's patrons into court for swearing – sometimes while they were actually inside the building. One August night in 1925, Constable Sawyer was walking past the saloon when he heard "indecent language" being used inside. He walked in and found Thomas Allen swearing. "There is no occasion to use such dirty language," the constable told him and it ended up costing Allen a £5 fine.

A year later, Stanley Plummer got done for swearing after dropping his hat in the saloon. In 1927, one Kenneth Payne was walking along the street and confronted a family coming the other way, all holding hands. Constable PE Bennett said as Payne tried to pass he was bumped against the wall of Sheppard's. That then caused Payne to lash out at the "Salvationists" (there was a Salvation Army hall across the road on the southwestern corner of Keira and Victoria streets), claiming they "put me out of my course".

Payne then walked around to the back of the saloon, Constable Bennett followed him to arrest him for indecent language. "Who to?" Payne asked. "Those Salvation Army people. You ought to be ashamed of yourself for using such filthy language." Payne then tried to suggest the man was a friend of his, though did not know his name. Like many others who frequented the billiard saloon, Payne walked away with a fine.

Hospital Hill

Hospital Hill wasn't always at its current location of Crown Street, west of the Denison Street intersection. It was once a whole lot closer to Keira Street; the rise of Flinders Street that meets the intersection of Keira and Smith was the first Hospital Hill. News stories in the late 1800s give it that name and, later, both they and business ads would refer to the "old Hospital Hill" and the "new Hospital Hill".

There wasn't some earthquake in the city's history that moved what we know as Hospital Hill closer to Keira Street, but rather that hill got its name for the fact that the first hospital was built in what is now the Collegians car park.

It was the Albert Memorial Hospital, usually referred to as the AM Hospital. It was built in memory of Prince Albert, who died in 1861, after locals had dismissed the idea of erecting a statue in his memory. To help fund the construction of the hospital, there was a call in the newspapers for subscribers to kick in some cash. In those articles, proponents explained why a hospital was needed (at the time sick people were treated at home).

"The necessity for some place where the sick and injured settlers and miners could be received and minded has long been apparent, especially when a severe accident has occurred," one such appeal read. "The medical attendant has laboured under great disadvantages in treating such a case at the home of the sufferer; and, at last he had sometimes been compelled to advise the removal of the patient to Sydney, that he may receive skilful nursing and the frequent visits of the surgeon."

It would be a "working man's hospital" the appeal claimed, and not some place of "refuge for the destitute or a home for the skulker".

It was a few years after Prince Albert's death before the foundation stone was laid – suggesting funds were hard to come by as the passion for some sort of memorial waned over time. That foundation stone was laid in June 1863, and the "modern Italian-style" plans for the hospital were publicly unveiled.

"The building is of brick, on a stone foundation," the *Illawarra Express* said. "There are two wing facades decorated with cement cornices. The plan embraces a centre building and two wings, which as wards, will suffice for the accommodation of about 20 patients.

"The front is to be erected first and when the central building is completed, then the wings are to be added. The portion of the building to be first erected will consist of waiting room, corridor, two six-bedded wards, store, pantry and linen closet, parlour, bedroom and kitchen."

Keira Street

The hospital was finally opened in September 1864 and would operate in a different fashion to what we expect of hospitals today. While emergency cases were always admitted, other patients could only be admitted under the authority of a subscriber who had donated money to help build the hospital. Those rules sometimes caused friction, as a Dr John Kerr recalled in a history piece published in the *South Coast Times* in 1954.

"I received a call late one cold, wet winter's night to the Cordeaux where a child lay seriously ill with diphtheria," Dr Kerr said. "I brought the child to the hospital and gave treatment by which she later recovered.

"The next day I was confronted by two committee members who asked me by what authority had I brought the child to the hospital."

The AM Hospital treated its last patient in 1908, and for the last decade there has been questions about the suitability of the site due to its proximity to the Mt Keira tramway (which took coal down to the harbour) and increasing traffic on what is now Flinders Street curtailing any expansion plans. After several years of planning, in 1906 a foundation stone was laid at the site of Wollongong Hospital, and when it was opened a year later, the area soon took over the name of "Hospital Hill"

For a time it seemed the old Hospital Hill was a perfect place for a hospital, if newspaper reports of people coming to grief on that incline are any indication. In 1897 local cycling champion Joseph Parsons was heading down the hill when a dog darted out in front of him. Parsons collided with the dog, fell off and broke his arm.

The *Mercury* reported that his bike "was considerably damaged".

Bert Harrigan was leaving work in Keira Street and somehow came off his bike while heading down the hill, injuring his face and elbow. "So heavy was the fall," the *Mercury* said, "that the boy lay in the AM Hospital the greater part of the night unconscious." The bike, which he had built himself, was "uninjured by the heavy fall".

Others had problems navigating the gate that blocked off the tramway when loads of coal were passing through. "The other day Mr FA Taylor, while riding his motor bicycle down the Hospital Hill, had to jump off and let the machine go in order to avert colliding with a train which had just emerged from the Keira gate," the *South Coast Times* reported.

"A lady cyclist lately had a similar experience. She turned her bicycle onto the bank of the footpath and had a painful fall. This is a crossing which evidently requires attention."

No report was given on the condition of their bikes.

Truck ablaze

The quick thinking of a truck driver heading down Keira Street averted an explosion in the Wollongong CBD in 1950.

Just after 8am on Saturday, September 16, William Schultz was driving his semi loaded up with nine tonnes of leather along Crown Street, having left Sydney on his way to Melbourne. Just as he turned right into Keira Street he heard the shouts from bystanders that there were flames coming from his truck. Fearing the harm that could come to pedestrians at the Crown Street intersection if he stopped and the petrol in the semi's tank exploded, Schultz drove on to the intersection with Burelli Street before he applied the brakes and jumped out.

By this time the truck was fully ablaze; the canvas canopy over the cabin where Schultz had been sitting seconds earlier was engulfed in flames. By the time the fire crews arrived, the flames were shooting 12 metres in the air. The fire-fighters quickly got the blaze under control, though the truck continued to smoulder.

"Apparently a drum of petrol which was stored between the cabin of the truck and the trailer was pierced by an iron trailer bar as I swung the corner," he said.

"I've been driving interstate trucks for six years and this is the first time I've ever experienced a fire. I hope it's the last time."

Trouser burglar

Wollongong police likely thought they'd nabbed the dreaded "trousers burglar" in Keira Street when he decided to rob one of their own.

As far as Wollongong true crime stories go, not much is said about the trousers burglar, but he was busy enough in the 1940s to warrant the media giving him a nickname. The burglar tended to focus on what is now considered the Wollongong CBD and surrounding suburbs.

In December 1940, the *Mercury* reported that he'd been at it in Smiths Hill, including a description of what he liked to do.

"His procedure is to enter a house in the early hours of the morning, enter the bedroom of the sleeping occupants and remove their clothing to the backyard, where he goes through the pockets," the *Mercury* reported.

While he tended to take cash and jewellery, he also had an odd fondness for a World War II item - petrol coupons.

The *Mercury*'s story suggested he kept himself busy; in one night the trousers burglar visited two houses in Kembla Street, one in Cliff Road and another in Wilson Street. In those thefts he took cash, jewellery – and yes – petrol coupons.

A week later he was at it again, stealing cash from the pockets of sleeping residents in several homes. Not even Christmas Eve 1940 was reason to take a break; he decided to poke around Dr Goldie's house, though there was no reports of what was stolen.

The police didn't like the man who represented the only blemish on their perfect record for 1940; the *Mercury* reported the trousers burglar was the only crime not cleared off the books by the end of the year.

In early January he was back in the Smiths Hill area, and the media reports went for a bit of victim-blaming. They suggested he liked the area because "the inmates of residences are more likely to be careless of money, and leave it in their trousers pocket than those in other portions of the town".

But on January 9, it looked like the cops had nabbed their man, after he was foolish enough to try and steal a detective's pants in Keira Street.

Detective JS Brown had just arrived in town on the Monday to take over the Wollongong detectives' bureau and was staying in a room at the Flinders Inn on the north-western corner of Keira and Crown streets.

Just four days later on the Thursday at around 11pm, the detective got changed in his room, put on his dressing gown and headed for the communal bathroom.

Keira Street

Now, you would think a lawman would know better, but Brown left the door to his room open. When he returned, he saw the door to another guest's room closing and then found his pants had been stolen.

He went in to question the resident, a John William Dickenson, who insisted he had no idea what happened to the pants. At that moment, a policeman was on patrol outside on Keira Street and found the pants on the footpath – directly below Dickenson's window. The cop then brought them up and handed over the pants.

Again the cops questioned Dickenson, who put himself in it by saying "I would not steal your trousers for a few lousy bob." That was the worst thing he could have said, because a few bob was exact amount of money the detective had in his trousers. And how would Dickenson have known that if he hadn't swiped the strides?

Dickenson's defence was that he had been at the Dapto dogs on the night in question and went straight to bed after arriving at the Flinders Inn. "I did not go into room 10 that night," he told the court. "I did not throw the trousers out the window. I did not touch them. I went straight to my room."

The judge thought it unlikely that a non-resident burglar was in the Flinders Inn at exactly the time Detective Brown arrived. He found Dickenson guilty and sentenced him to two months in prison.

Was he the trousers bandit? Well, he suggested he had been working in Darwin for months before arriving in Wollongong in January.

But on the other hand, there were no media reports of

the trouser burglar's adventures while Dickenson was in jail. So maybe he was the trouser burglar. And maybe he got away with it.

Alwyn Hardie

On the afternoon of June 17, 1935, Alwyn Hardie was in Keira Street, making his way home. He still had some way to go; he lived down Gladstone Avenue which was a good half-kilometre away. It seems 1935 was a very different time, for Alwyn was just six years old and he was walking home from school.

Where he went to school wasn't clear but his route, via Smith and then Keira streets was certainly the long way to get to Gladstone Avenue. What his thinking was will forever remain a mystery, as would what he did while on Keira Street. When Hardie got onto Keira Street he chose to go on the road and run along behind a car heading south.

As he neared the Market Street intersection, Hardie ran out from behind the car and into the side of a lorry travelling in the opposite direction. The driver, Herbert Murray, stopped immediately and got out, seeing the body of the boy under one of the wheels. An ambulance arrived and took Hardie to hospital suffering a fractured skull but he died shortly after being admitted.

The coroner later said Murray was blameless and it was a case of accidental death. "The fatality was an illustration of the need for the public co-operating with the police and the school authorities in their endeavours to educate the children regarding the danger of motor traffic," the *Mercury* reported.

Murray told the coroner that the schoolchildren at Unanderra were the worst. They spread out all over the road, he said, and would not get out of the way when a motor vehicle approached. The coroner identified several "death traps" in the city – none of which were the Keira-Market street intersection where Hardie died. He said the bridges and level crossings of the Keira line that was used to transport coal to the harbour were terrible.

"Wollongong council should endeavour to get the railway department to have a footbridge constructed on the bridges," he said, "or traffic lines painted, where the children would be free from the dangers of motor vehicles."

Sunday drinking

The long trek from Mt Pleasant to Wollongong was one that certainly required a beer. Or at least that's what several drinkers told the court after being busted in the Royal Alfred Hotel on the northeastern corner of Keira and Crown streets on a Sunday.

Back in 1876, the idea of being in a bar on the Sabbath was illegal; unless you were a traveller. That was the loophole through which the four men nabbed by Senior Sergeant Sheridan were hoping to crawl. On that Sunday morning, between 10 and 11am, Sgt Sheridan was on the corner when he heard some noises coming from the Royal Alfred.

He went around to the back door and found George Duffy behind the bar serving drinks to four men – AH Ritchie, J Smith, W Frost and M Smith. Sheridan tasted one of the drinks in front of the men and found it to be porter. He booked the lot of them, insisting there was no mileage limit stated in the legislation and, given Mt Pleasant was only two miles away, it was ridiculous to suggest they were travellers. If they'd come from Campbelltown or Kiama, well that would have been a different matter altogether.

Ritchie and both Smiths mounted a defence that claimed there was nothing else other than beer available to a thirsty traveller from Mt Pleasant. "They said the forenoon in question being very hot and the walk having made them very heated and thirsty," the *Mercury* reported, "they went into a hotel m as they thought they had a perfect right to do.

"There was no water along the road for them to drink, and the water even where they resided at Mt Pleasant was so bad as to be unfit for use."

Surely, they said, the judge wouldn't have wanted them to die of thirst on the roadside, forcing a coroner to carry out an investigation. "All they required and all they asked for was a drink to quench their thirst," the paper reported, "a thing they could not go and ask for in a private place." And then after that drink they'd planned to go to church, which was the reason they traipsed into town from Mt Pleasant in the first place.

The judge wasn't swayed by their pleas; he fined all four men five shillings, while Duffy had to pay a pound for serving them.

Shots fired

The sound of gunfire in Keira Street has been slightly more common that one might think. And the same man – nightwatchman John McCloskey – was responsible for two of those incidents.

In June 1937 McCloskey – who had been hired by the Wollongong Traders Association to watch over their buildings at night – was on patrol on Crown Street. Just after midnight on Friday, June 11, he spotted a man trying to break through the front door of Marcus Clarke's on the corner of Crown and Atchison streets.

When he reached the front door, McCloskey noticed the jemmy marks on the door and that the padlock had been removed. But McCloskey couldn't apprehend the man he'd seen, who had disappeared down Atchison Street. Instead the nightwatchman went to the store manager's house – a Mr Henlen – to let them know what was happening.

When he returned to the store, McCloskey saw the man was back. Searching him, he found the man was carrying a spanner and a torch but claimed to know nothing at all about the missing padlock. The nightwatchman then arrested him and let the man know they were going to the police station. The nightwatchman then started pulling the man towards the police station.

By this time, Mr Henlen had made his way to the store and then joined the nightwatchman and the crim on their walk to the law. When the trio reached the intersection of Keira and Crown streets, the burglar pushed over the store manager and made a run for it down Keira Street. McCloskey drew his gun and fired two shots at the fleeing man and then gave chase into Burelli Street. Running through Rest Park, McCloskey let off four more shots before the chase continued up Globe Lane, into Crown Street and then back down Church Street, where the man disappeared.

McCloskey would give two different descriptions of the chase – the above one that he told the court and one he told the *Mercury* the day of the incident, where he claimed all six shots were let loose in Burelli Street. The court version seems more likely; it's hard to fathom that the crim could have run all the way from the Keira-Crown intersection and into Burelli before the nightwatchman fired the first shot. Also, as we will soon see, McCloskey seemingly had no concern about firing off a few rounds at a suspect.

By this time, the police had heard the gunfire and went out to see what was going on. They soon discovered a man hiding in in the rear yard of the nearby Blue Ribbon Café in Crown Street. McCloskey immediately identified

Keira Street

him as the man he was chasing.

In court later that month, the man was identified as 26-year-old Port Kembla steelworker Frederick Ellis. But the attempted break-in at Marcus Clarke's wasn't all he was charged with; Ellis had been a very busy man indeed.

He was also charged with stealing a car horn from Darlinghurst, some grease guns from a Sydney garage, a range of car accessories at Flemington and a dinner suit he found in the back of a car.

In Wollongong, he had also broken into a tailor in Central Chambers – in the lower half of the Crown Street mall – four nights earlier and stolen some material, a jacket and two pairs of trousers. That last one was hard for Ellis to argue, he was actually wearing a pair of those trousers when the police arrested him on the morning of June 11.

But it goes on; Ellis had also broken into the same tailor a week earlier, snaffling an overcoat. He'd also stolen a lumber jacket from Baxter's clothing store in Central Chambers.

The police decided to drop some of the charges, perhaps figuring Ellis was going to go off to prison for a while anyway. And he did – Ellis spent more than a year in jail.

Almost exactly a year earlier, nightwatchman McCloskey was in court over an incident that saw him fire his gun on Keira Street. At 4am on June 6, 1936, Edward Martin, one of McCloskey's fellow nightwatchmen, had seen a man ride a bike away from the warehouse of CA Penny on the corner of Keira and Smith streets.

Curious, Martin went to the Smith Street door and tried to open it but it felt like someone was on the other side holding it closed. He then made his way around to the Keira Street entrance, where he saw McCloskey. The nightwatchmen conferred; with McCloskey telling Martin to go and re-examine all the doors and windows.

He did that and then headed along Keira Street towards Crown Street, looking for a policeman on patrol. While Martin was away, McCloskey later testified that he saw the suspect at the top of the stairs in the warehouse. He told the man he was going to be arrested, but the man swung an iron bar he was holding at McCloskey's head and ran off.

The nightwatchman fired two shots over the man's head but he didn't stop, so two more shots were fired at his legs, which brought him down. At this point Martin returned with Constable Wilson to find McCloskey standing over the prone body of the man around 40 metres from the Keira-Smith street corner.

"Did you shoot him, Mac," Martin asked.

"I had to or he would have gotten away," McCloskey replied.

The constable and the nightwatchmen later entered the warehouse, finding papers strewn everywhere and gelignite attached to a safe in the office.

On June 17, Harold Maher was carried into Wollongong Police Court on a stretcher to hear the charges against him. Maher had been taken to hospital after being shot in the legs. While there, police searched his trousers, finding gelignite and wool in the pockets.

Constable Wilson told the court Maher had admitted in hospital that he had been in Penny's warehouse and, later, that jemmy bars found inside were his.

Maher chose not to say anything and so was committed to stand trial on the breaking and entering charge and another of carrying a firearm, which had been in his pocket at the time (though why he opted not to fire back at McCloskey was unknown). A further charge of stealing the gun from a Nowra garage was dismissed.

In the trial of July 22, Maher – who hobbled into court on crutches – pleaded guilty to both charges. Judge Curlewis then heard a long list of stealing convictions Maher had in Queensland. Curlewis appeared more concerned with the gun in Maher's pocket than the attempted break-in with the gelignite.

"What were you doing with a pistol in your possession?" he asked Maher.

"I was trying to raise a few shillings on it. I bought it three months ago."

"You carried it about with you for three months and you admit during that period it was fully loaded."

Then the judge had a dig at Maher's crutches.

"I also noticed that you came into court on two crutches. The doctor reports that you can walk without them."

"I still have a bullet in my leg," Maher replied, perhaps with some justification.

Maher and his crutches were sent to jail for four years. Judge Curlewis was so unimpressed with the fact he had been carrying around a gun that he refused a request from

Maher's lawyer that his time be reduced in the event of good conduct. Nor would the judge count the weeks he had already spent in custody as part of his sentence.

Crash

It was only after Reginald Parry hit the woman with his car that he realised he knew her. On the night of Friday, September 8, 1934, Parry was in his car, driving north along Keira Street. He planned to turn right into Market Street and, in an era where the intersection was not controlled by traffic lights, he had to wait for an oncoming vehicle to pass before making his turn.

The lighting at the intersection was poor and, as Parry turned into Market Street a woman appeared in his vision from behind the car that had just passed. He hit the brakes but there was no time to pull up; his car hit the woman in the chest, knocking her onto the road. She hit the back of her head on the road surface.

Constable Lyons was one of several witnesses who gave evidence to the coroner, saying he had passed the woman on Market Street about 10 metres before she got to the intersection. "A few seconds later I heard a scream and turned sharply and saw the form of a woman falling in front of a motor car," the constable told the court.

Together with Parry, the constable moved the woman and it was then he recognised her as Florence Potts. When he mentioned it to Parry, the driver realised with a shock, he had known her when they both lived in Lithgow; his family and hers were quite friendly.

The constable felt Parry had done all he could to avoid the accident, adding there was an issue with the lighting at that section of Keira Street and also that Potts was short-sighted and may not have even seen Parry's car before crossing.

Also close to the scene was Dr Lee, whom the constable had called out to for assistance. Looking at Mrs Potts briefly, Dr Lee ordered her to be taken to Wollongong Hospital. Once there a closer inspection showed Mrs Potts had a fractured skull, most likely caused when her head hit the road. There were no other injuries, nor was there any sign that Parry's car had driven over her.

Mrs Potts died in hospital on the Saturday morning. To heighten the tragedy, that very day her son had come down from Lithgow to see his family. Instead, he ended up at the hospital morgue, where he had to identify his mother's body.

In the coroner's court, Dr Lee said that he had not heard any sound before the accident which indicated to him that Parry was not driving fast; in fact he felt no driver could make that turn at any speed.

Other witnesses supported the claim that Parry did all he could and so the coroner gave a finding of accidental death with no blame affixed to Parry.

Quattro

If you stand at the Smith Street intersection and look to the north, you can see the towers of the Parq on Flinders apartment complex. The site upon which they sit was the spark that lit the 2008 corruption scandal that gave the city of Wollongong a black eye and became the source of many salacious headlines.

In the mix was a plastic table and chairs outside of a North Wollongong kebab shop, where those who sat there anointed themselves the city's movers and shakers. They even named the plastic setting the Table of Knowledge, which probably sounded funny at the time but looked tacky when it made the papers. There were also conmen who tricked some city councillors into believing they were investigators with the Independent Commission Against Corruption. They allegedly told the councillors they had incriminating photos of them meeting with developers and that, for a fee, the conmen could make the evidence disappear.

At the heart of the sex and corruption scandal was

developer Frank Vellar's ambitious Quattro development that was to sit on the block of Flinders, Campbell and Keira streets. With four towers, 17 storeys and 276 apartments it broke a number of planning rules. It was to be 48 metres high in a precinct where the maximum height was 11 metres, its floor-space ratio was out of whack and those 17 storeys were 11 more than the rules allowed.

Yet, in August 2005 it was approved – by a town planner who was sleeping with Vellar. Beth Morgan had started hanging out with Vellar and the other members of the arrogantly-named Table of Knowledge in March 2004, just four weeks after she'd returned from maternity leave to her town planning job at Wollongong City Council. Sometimes she even brought her baby daughter to the table on chilly mornings.

In an email to a work colleague she explained her motivations were fuelled by a desire to make connections with developers like Vellar and Glen Tabak, who also had a seat at the table. Once she left the council, she told the workmate, her family's future would be dependent on good relationships with them.

"Don't think for a second that I am not going to do what I need to do to ensure their survival," she wrote in the email.

That apparently included the married town planner sleeping with the married developer. Four weeks after she sat at the Table of Knowledge Morgan was in bed with Vellar. By July 2004, Vellar had requested council general manager Rod Oxley appoint Morgan to his Quattro proposal. His request was granted.

During the approval process, Vellar showered her with perfume, flowers, handbags, wine, cash and even a holiday. In return Morgan forwarded on the public objections to Quattro to her lover and aimed to see the massive development got through the council.

Some council staff got suspicious and thought Morgan was sleeping with Vellar, though she denied it to her manager and to a work colleague. We're just friends, she told them.

Before the project was approved the council's planning director David Broyd quit – in part because of what he told ICAC was Oxley's "high-level interference" when planning staff were carrying out their duties and directing them to change their positions on planning matters. Broyd told ICAC it was called "the level 10 factor", a reference to the location of Oxley's office. When he quit, the responsibility for the Quattro approval largely fell in Morgan's lap. And so, on August 18, 2005, she approved it. The only reason it wasn't built before the corruption scandal broke in 2008 was that Vellar hadn't obtained a construction certificate; if he'd managed that, the view north from the Smith Street intersection would be very, very different.

Still, the development approval Morgan granted in 2005 was live. It was live in December 2006 when ICAC investigators raided the council building. It was live in February 2008 when the ICAC hearings began. And it wouldn't lapse until August 18, 2008.

Once granted, approvals are very hard to reverse. But

the council found a loophole; it could be overturned if the council could prove it had been "tainted" by corruption. Seemed that should be pretty easy to prove, so in March the council took Vellar to the Land and Environment Court. In June, ICAC helped immensely by handing down an interim report that said Morgan and Vellar engaged in "serious corrupt conduct". The court granted a halt on any Quattro work and in early 2009 overturned the approval – and slugged Vellar with the council's court costs.

That meant the council administrators – the council itself had been sacked in the wake of the ICAC case - could reassess it and reject it, which they obviously did. But they also said Vellar could still build Quattro, as long as he scaled it back to fit the planning limits for the site. That never happened and, in 2010, Vellar's company went into administration and a fire sale of the properties he had took place. It was a sale some credit with the rejuvenation of the city as it freed up land that had been sitting in limbo for years.

So sites like Langs Corner and the old indoor cricket centre at Fairy Meadow were sold, as was the massive Quattro block. Oddly, the buyer for the Quattro site was the council itself, which picked it up in November 2011 for $5.2 million and planned to turn much of it into a car park – a far cry from earlier talk that it could serve as a "gateway" entry to the city. Though there were still hope something could come after the car park – which the council insisted was only a temporary measure.

"The council sees this site as a really important

gateway to the city," said the council's property manager Peter Coyte. "Our aim is to clean it up and make it as impressive as we can in the short-to-medium term."

But in April 2012, the car park plans had been shelved and the council had the site on the market. It was bought by a consortium of Malaysian investors with grand plans to include trendy restaurants and an arthouse cinema, along with apartments. Those plans would be wound back, in part because of the project's soaring 60-metre building height.

The revised project included 221 apartments across four towers and some ground floor commercial space – and was known as Parq on Flinders. It was approved in 2016 and, unlike the infamous Quattro, construction work actually started and the project was completed by late 2020.

As for the fallout from that ICAC scandal, it was a bit of a fizzer. The body made corrupt conduct findings against Morgan and Vellar, as well as Oxley, four city councillors and three others. But only one of those 10 people saw any jail time – city councillor Frank Gigliotti. Vellar was also found guilty – of three charges of giving false evidence and one count of fabricating a document – but got to serve his 10-month sentence in the community via an intensive correctional order. The only other person found guilty in court was developer Tabak, who was fined $2500 and placed on a two-year good behaviour bond for making a false statement to ICAC

Other councillors Kiril Jonovski and Zeki Esen were both found not guilty in court of giving false evidence, while no charges were pursued against Cr Val Zanotto due to a lack of evidence. ICAC did not recommend charging Oxley, despite making a corrupt conduct finding against him.

Even though ICAC recommended Morgan face 27 charges over misconduct in public office, receiving gifts and benefits from developers and misleading ICAC, she walked. The DPP said there was insufficient "admissible" evidence to prosecute her. And with that the DPP closed the files on the corruption scandal.

Many in the city would have agreed with the *Mercury*'s editorial on that day.

"The scandal, it seemed, had everything, except justice for the people of Wollongong – who this morning discovered the DPP has closed the case.

"It means that some of the main players, in particular Beth Morgan, will never have their day in court.

"Wollongong has every right to feel cheated."

Dynamite

Just before lunchtime on August 28, 2012, a loud bang echoed along Keira Street and rocks flew across the Crown Street intersection. "A lot of people came out into the street," said Colin Hughes, who owned a Keira Street business just south of Crown Street. "I don't think anybody really knew what it was. I think people were expecting to see a car crash or something."

He went outside and found a rock the size of his fist in the middle of the road. It wasn't a car crash, but rather an explosion at the GPT's Wollongong Central site, which was still under excavation. A method to break up the rock had been used - and things didn't quite go according to plan.

"We tested a method called bedrock fracturing" GPT group development manager Steve Turner said, "in order to loosen the bedrock with the aim of speeding up its excavation, which involved a small explosion being used to loosen the bedrock.

"Although the methodology was sound, unfortunately

the rock reacted in a manner that was different from what experts in this field had expected. Some rock left the boundary of the building site."

The method would not be used again, Mr Turner said.

But it was easy to see why it was trialled – the rock that had to be excavated was extremely unco-operative when it came to being removed. Drilling had gone on for more than a year, with 600 cubic metres of rock excavated every day. Residents in apartments immediately west of the site had to deal with the daily noise and GPT even had to take over the lease of a nearby business where the excavation work was about to get underway right next-door. The group also had to spring for 30 car covers for vehicles parking immediately north of the site to deal with the dust that had been kicked up.

The excavation work was supposed to be completed by February 2013, but it wasn't until April that the drilling rigs finally fell silent. Later, when the centre was opened, Mr Turner said the slab underneath the shopping centre was "widely recognised as being the hardest rock in Australia".

"The excavation went longer than it was supposed to and it was a lot higher impact than we wanted it to be," he said.

"For some particular reason the rock on this site was so uniform in its creation and hardly any fractures or seams to help you break it up. We'd seen other people dig through the same kind of rock, and multiple contractors gave us advice on what the program would be and how long it would take – and everyone was wrong."

Remembering a tragedy

In the early afternoon of July 31, 1902, heads in the city turned to the west. A large boom had echoed out from Mt Kembla, and a huge volume of smoke could be seen emanating from the mine. The telegraph quickly brought news of a tragedy – there had been an explosion in the mine, while both shifts were below ground.

"In a short space of time the road to Kembla was dotted with men hurrying forward – on horseback, on bicycles or in vehicles," the *South Coast Times* reported. "Distressed women, dragging children after them, were passed, but nothing authentic was learnt until arrival at Kembla Heights."

Once there, those who had rushed up the mountain to the mine were greeted with a horrible sight. "The main entrance was completely blocked up and the engine-house wrecked," the *Times* said. "Huge pieces of timber and bars of iron were respectively splintered or twisted into every variety of fantastic shape. Sheets of galvanised iron were suspended from tops of trees several hundred yards away."

The *Illawarra Mercury* told of mothers, daughters and sons rushing to the mouth of the tunnel, only to be turned back by the smoke still pouring from the mine and the blanched faces of the men still above ground.

"The screams of the women and children were heartrending," the *Mercury* wrote. "They felt certain, seeing the fearful outpouring of smoke and the ominous silence of the telephone which runs about two miles into the mine, that the explosion had smashed the wires and possibly caused the roof of the tunnel to collapse, thus making the men prisoners, and perhaps killing many of them."

An inquiry would later rule the tragedy was set in motion by the collapse of a large section of the mine roof, which pushed air and methane gas into the main tunnel. That rush of air and gas stirred up coal dust, which made contact with an exposed flame, creating ignition and blowing a fireball down the tunnel. A chain reaction of explosions followed, giving the miners underground no warning or chance to escape. Many of those who survived the flames succumbed to the carbon monoxide gas left behind.

At the time of the explosion, 261 men were in the mine. The final death toll would be 96 miners, some of them as young as 14. Also among the 96 were several of the rescuers; two of whom would be remembered on a memorial eventually set up on Crown Street, visible from the Keira Street corner. They were Major Henry MacCabe and William McMurray. The pair were part of a group who rushed into the mine to look for survivors. They were soon overcome by gas and made a retreat, some carrying the prone body of MacCabe, who told them to put him down and save themselves. When his body was found several hours later, he was clasped in the arms of McMurray, who had also died.

While many families lost loved ones that day, the deaths of the two rescuers resonated in the city. So much so that, a year later in August, the unveiling of a photo of Major MacCabe was significant enough to draw a large crowd to the Keiraville Mechanics Institute. "They all remembered with sorrow the dreadful time just 12 months ago where there was so much sadness throughout the district," the *Mercury* reported of the crowd, "and when Major MacCabe and William McMurray risked their lives in a noble endeavour to save the lives of their fellow men. They all felt that such deeds left the young nation of Australia richer than it would otherwise have been."

Later that month, it was decided that a photo was not enough to immortalise their efforts – as well as the lives of those miners who perished. And so a fund for a public memorial was created, with those who donated calling a meeting to decide where it should be located.

Initially, the plan was to erect it on the corner of Keira and Crown streets, though it would ultimately end up a few metres back, on the junction of Crown Street and Crown Lane. Photos show it sitting in the middle of Crown Lane, suggesting traffic was not so heavy at the time that it created an obstruction.

Though it took some time to get there - some felt it

belonged on Church Street between the church and what is now the mall. However, some objected to that location, fearing a runaway horse and cart on that downhill stretch could hit it. They felt it was better placed in front of the Town Hall.

But by August 1905, the Crown Street-Crown Lane option was finalised. The memorial, which included a pair of gas-powered lights and, reportedly, a fountain (though no photos show such a thing) was officially unveiled on August 19, 1905, in front of a crowd of around 5000 people in Keira and Crown streets.

There it remained until February 25, 1937, when the *Mercury* reported it was removed "without any ceremony" with plans to reinstall it at Wollongong Rest Park a month later. Ultimately it ended up – minus the hanging gas lights at the top – at the Soldiers and Miners Memorial Church in Mt Kembla

City living

These days, the idea of living on Keira Street is pretty difficult. One of the few places where it might still happen is the National Mutual Life Association building on the north-eastern corner with Market Street – the one with the clock at the top. There was a time when the upper floors were rented out but I'm not sure if that is still the case.

But before the street became a commercial strip, it was a place people called home. One example of that still stands – the house that is now occupied by Rookie Eatery and has been home to a number of restaurants before that. Who may have lived there is unclear but if the *Mercury* classifieds are any indication, it was inhabited as recently as 1954. That was when the resident placed an ad looking to offload a lady's bicycle for the princely sum of £8. In 1931, the resident there was wealthy enough to own a second property, in Denison Street, which they had up for rent.

A year later, there was a Mr Heininger living there and

he wanted to let everyone know he had a car for hire "day or night". In 1935, Mr Heininger had passed away and the home was up for sale; the ad described it as a "compact cottage home" with two bedrooms, a dining room and a large kitchen and a garage (presumably where that car for hire was parked).

In 1938 the last ad before that bicycle sale appeared – whoever bought Mr Heininger's house wanted to sell a pair of trucks – a Ford and a Dodge – at £20 and £30 respectively.

In 1952 Michael Mitchell was living at 134 Keira Street – on the Victoria Street corner. His address made the paper because someone broke into his house in the afternoon and stole two pairs of pants - whether that was the infamous trouser burglar written about elsewhere is unknown.

The Pinch family lived at 120 Keira Street and the 21st birthday of their son Ronald Thomas (known as Tommy) was so important that the *South Coast Times* covered it in 1940. Tommy got "a number of many valuable presents including a substantial wallet of notes from his parents". Nine years later, the Pinches must have moved out because Barry Lennon had moved in and proceeded to make himself known to police. In 1949 he was found guilty of causing "undue noise" on a motorcycle. A year later he was back again over the noisy motorbike and for riding without headlights. In 1953 he was sentenced to three months jail for stealing £25, though released on a good behaviour bond. Seems he'd sold someone's motorbike for them for £45 but only gave the owner £20.

Keira Street

In 1954 an unnamed tenant at 120 Keira Street – who was possibly Lennon – was evicted by court order after falling £213 behind in rent. That would have taken some doing given rent was £6 a week.

In recent times, there was the possibility of seeing people living on the CBD strip of Keira Street once again. In 2012 images of the Wollongong Central were released that showed two towers on top of the shopping centre. They were released by Wollongong City Council in a document about al fresco dining on the strip,

Steven Turner, GPT's development manager said there was no firm plans to build anything on top – but there might come a day when it lent itself to student accommodation or offices.

"It is public knowledge that GPT remains in discussions with the university in relation to the development of a student accommodation building," Turner said.

"GPT has identified that the city has a drastic shortage of both A-grade commercial office space as well as student accommodation. The plans shown [in the council document] are one potential response to meeting the immediate needs of the city. Given the unique location of the site there might be a range of uses."

An easier trip

For decades Keira Street was part of the reason travelling through the CBD was a pain in the backside. Sure, the mall was the main reason, but that transit mall between Crown and Burelli streets didn't help matters. Anyone travelling from the north hit the Keira and Crown intersection and was sent hurtling out to the west along Crown Street, turning into Atchison and then Burelli. Northbound traffic from Burelli Street had it tougher as Atchison Street was one-way, so they had to travel around two city blocks to get out. It was a dumb idea especially considering the main CBD car park was on the Burelli Street corner but everyone had to go the long way around to get there.

That section of Keira Street was closed to all but buses, taxis and delivery vans in 1985. It had been planned as part of a rescue package for the city after the steelworks crashed. The way it was figured at the time was to improve public transport in and out of the city by creating a dedicated transit mall along that section. It was meant to improve the bus flow along that section, where they had previously been caught up in a long line of cars. But over time, that good idea turned very bad as the numbers of buses in the city increased, as did the rest of the CBD traffic.

So the process of re-opening that stretch to all began, but it was far from quick. The city's business chamber, along with a group called Future Directions, included it in their plan to fix up the CBD in 2000. And the bus drivers *hated* it. Transport Workers Union branch secretary Don Clode said their members wouldn't drive a bus into the city if that happened.

"If this goes ahead, we will terminate buses at Gladstone Ave, JJ Kelly Park and at North Wollongong," Clode said. "Bus drivers already have a problem with pedestrians in that area between Keira and Burelli streets. Bringing in cars would cause a major bottleneck and make it extremely dangerous."

Future Directions chair Mark McDonald was not impressed, claiming the union was "holding the city to ransom". "The Keira Street reopening is only a tiny part of a major submission and it is unhelpful for the TWU to go off half-cocked and uninformed."

In 2001 council general manager Rod Oxley said it had to happen, but then it didn't happen for another nine years. It wasn't until 2010, with Oxley gone and administrators in charge of things, that there was action. The traffic change would cost $1.7 million and was part of a $17.8 million package zhoosh up the CBD – that included getting rid of the very-1980s birdcage in the mall.

The plan was to move the buses out of the transit mall first and into new stops on Crown, Burelli and Keira streets, the second step was to welcome southbound traffic and then northbound drivers a few months later.

In preparation for that first stage, Wollongong got its first dedicated bus lane – in Keira Street – and the walk signal at the lights at the top of the mall were changed so pedestrians could cross in any direction. Moving the buses out hit a snag with the council drawing criticism for leaving it until five days before the changeover to release maps to the public showing the new bus stops. "It should have been out a couple of weeks earlier to alert people this change was coming," said Dions Bus Service boss Les Dion.

Council GM David Farmer said releasing details of the colour co-ordinated stops that early would have caused too much confusion. As it was there were the evitable teething problems and grumbles from some commuters who had to walk an extra hundred metres to their new stop. Though there were valid gripes about the lack of any seating at the new CBD bus stops. Those seats would be installed in the coming weeks the council said, suggesting the maps weren't the only thing they left 'til the last minute.

The opening to southbound traffic, planned for June, was pushed back to December when the road would be opened in both directions. The need to include feedback from the Roads and Traffic Authority was blamed for the change of plan. Still CEO Farmer could see the benefits

Keira Street

of reopening the road. "This is especially important for visitors arriving in Wollongong from the north, who are currently sent west, away from the heart of the CBD," he said. "The opening of Keira Street will allow them to directly access the major parking stations in Kenny and Keira streets."

There would be a few rules car drivers would have to know. There would be no right turn from Keira into Burelli; with that section effectively one lane, a right-turning vehicle would create gridlock. And they'd need to get around how to behave near a bus lane – stay out of it unless going around a turning vehicle. That last one still caused confusion when the transit mall was reopened on Monday, November 29. Traffic banked up all the way to the Flinders Street intersection on that first day, as people didn't want to stray into the bus lane, or simply didn't realise that they could continue travelling along Keira Street.

A few pedestrians nearly got skittled too after forgetting the Crown-Burelli section of Keira Street now had a lot more traffic on it.

Bruce Gordon's Grand plan

Bruce Gordon was playing the long game. It was like a decades-long version of Monopoly. It started back in 1990 when the billionaire and WIN TV boss bought The Grand Hotel. A year later, he became the owner of the NRMA Building on the corner of Crown and Keira streets after plonking down $2.85 million. Around the same time he bought two other Crown Street properties for about $2 million combined.

Later, in 2015 he got the former Commonwealth Bank building and the IMB head office for $12 million. He kept on snapping up properties on the block bordered by Keira, Crown, Atchison and Burelli streets until he grabbed the last one – the medical centre on Crown Street – in 2021. It was after that purchase that Gordon unveiled his master plan, just over two decades in the making. A $400 million project called WIN Grand. The "Grand" name came from the hotel, the first property he acquired. But it could just have easily been a description of the development, because $400 million buys a lot of stuff to fill up a whole city block.

It included three separate residential towers, a cinema and 600-person capacity music venue where the Grand sat (even keeping the original facade) office space, a gym and a swimming pool. "Bruce is trying to really plug some of the gaps in the city," said development director Steven Turner (the man behind Wollongong Central) "making sure that we're not competing with what's already in the city but we're complementing it."

With all that space to play with, to fill up with the real-life equivalent of Monopoly's green houses and red hotels (though, technically, neither houses or hotels featured) Turner decided to start with a footpath. Pedestrians know well the slopes of Keira and Atchison; heading downhill is easy, walking up into the CBD, not so much. But after surveying the block, it was discovered that the Keira-Crown and Burelli-Atchison corners were somehow at the same level. The corners on the other diagonal had a 10-metre fall. Weird, huh?

Turner saw this as an option to create a better pedestrian route between the train station and the mall – right through the middle of the WIN Grand block. "That was the first thing that got stuck on the drawing," Turner said. "It got drawn in and it never left the project. Then it got made more interesting, because no-one wants to generally walk through a straight line – that might be the shortest route but it doesn't make it the best route.

"So we worked out how to bring that through the site and make it interesting, taking corners and keeping people engaged through there. But you still get that flat walk, which is amazing."

The local council was a big fan; they had been using this new phrase "night-time economy" whenever it came to the CBD and figured this development would be a boost to whatever happened when the sun went down. "The idea being that this will spill over and energise the nightlife," Lord Mayor Gordon Bradbery said, "and will become an attractor, not only for those who live in that space but also for those who journey into the centre of Wollongong – seeing it as a hub for entertainment services and hospitality and those sorts of things."

Not everyone was a fan of Bruce Gordon's Grand plan. Some were not impressed with the height of the apartment towers – one of which was higher than allowed in the area. Others focused on the issue that, despite the presence of a music venue, gym, theatre and more to attract the general public, there was no parking created for them. Instead, those people could just park over the road at Wollongong Central, which owner GPT thought was quite a cheeky move indeed. There had also long been the belief that more people will use public transport to get into the city, negating the need for parking spaces. Yet, despite people talking that up, it was a dream that had yet to come true.

The objections didn't get in the way of the project getting approved by the regional planning panel, who could handle the too-tall tower and the parking issues. In fact, it felt the final design was better than if they'd had to adhere to the rules.

In mid-2023, Gordon's investment company Birketu

was looking for a developer to partner up with. And fair enough – someone had to actually build the thing. About eight months later, that partner had become a purchaser, with Sydney developer Level 33 snapping up the city block for a cool $70 million, making it the biggest single real estate transaction in the CBD's history.

"I don't think the intention was to sell it [from the start]," said Colliers Simon Kersten, who oversaw the search for a partner. "I think the intention was to build it. But obviously things change, it took some time for the DA to get approved and then Bruce made a decision that he wanted somebody else to take it over.

"A half-a-billion dollar real estate development is not something that anyone wants to take lightly."

Indeed.

The Grand Hotel

In the 1930s, the population was growing so fast that the city was running out of places to put them. Men were heading to Wollongong for jobs at the steelworks and needed somewhere to sleep. The situation was so dire that, according to Sydney paper, *Smith's Weekly*, multiple steelworkers were sharing the few beds in hotels and hostels in shifts. One would finish work and crash but need to be up and out by the time the next person ended their shift at the steelworks.

A *Smith's Weekly* journo was sent to Wollongong for a story and was unaware of the accommodation crisis. "About 10pm he decided to take a room at a hotel, but a round of the leading hotels resulted in nothing but an apology from proprietors, apparently astonished at the existence of such an optimist," the *Weekly* wrote.

"From the last hotel, *Smith's* was directed to a boarding house, where the landlady offered a bed on condition that it should not be used before 11.30pm – as one of the 'steelies' was sleeping out his shift. It was a further condition that the bed should be vacated by 7am, so that another home-coming worker should be accommodated."

That boarding house had 15 rooms, with 53 men living there. Other steelworkers couldn't find accommodation close to work and ended up bedding down more than 40 kilometres away and having to rely on public transport to make it to work.

This shortage prompted the construction of two new hotels on Keira Street – the Grand Hotel and the Illawarra Hotel – both with accommodation upstairs. The Grand got its doors open first in 1937, a year earlier than the Illawarra Hotel. The pub's licence was held by the Welch family, who had first used it at the Grenadier Hotel at Otford when the Otford tunnel was being excavated in the 1880s. In 1886, with the tunnel complete, the licence moved to Paragon Hotel at Helensburgh, where the mine had just started. The family kept it there until the kate 1930s, when it was transferred to the Grand.

The Grand was officially opened with a luncheon on Monday, November 29, 1937. "This very fine hotel is designed on modern lines with elegant appointments," the *South Coast Times* wrote of the opening, "and smart furnishings, embodying every conceivable feature to make the life of the guest homelike and enjoyable."

On hand to officially open the Grand was state Labor MP Billy Davies who said the new hotel – built on the site of a blacksmith's shop – was a sign of the growing city. *The Mercury* provided a summary of Davies' comments. "During the past 12 months, the population had increased by 3000 adults. There were signs of progress on every hand. Wollongong Theatres was expending £10,000 in bringing the Crown Theatre up to date and contemplated erecting another theatre, not far from the site of the Crown Hotel. The council would have to open up Burelli Street to the railway station."

Truthfully, Davies was an odd choice to open up the Grand. Sure, he lived next-door but had been having a stoush with the Grand's builders over excavation work, which had exposed the foundations of the two-storey building in which he and his wife lived. Just six months before the grand opening, the builder had been taken to court by the city council and fined £5 for not shoring up the Davies' wall.

In May 1938, Davies himself took the builders to court, looking to get them to cough up £2000. "Plaintiff alleged that the defendants wrongfully dug out and removed certain land adjacent to the land/houses and buildings of the plaintiff," the *Mercury* reported during that case, "without shoring up, or underpinning the houses and buildings. Plaintiff alleged that this had caused his land, houses, and buildings to sink and give way, that the buildings were cracked and injured, and were greatly depreciated in value."

At the end of the six-day hearing, Davies won but got far less than he wanted; the court awarded him £641.

Given that it was a pub, it wasn't surprising that it regularly appeared in the papers over claims of illegal betting going on and the supply of booze outside the six o'clock swill era legislation. One amusing example of the latter happened in June 1938 when Constable Chalker was in a police car tooling along Burelli Street on a Saturday night, when he saw Albert Collings walk out of The Grand cradling a bottle of beer (the main entrance to the pub was originally on Burelli Street). Before the police could apprehend Collings, he walked across the road, placed the bottle on the steps of the Crown Theatre and then sprinted up Keira Street.

When caught, Collings offered the weak defence of "that's not my bottle, I've never seen it before", which wasn't assisted by his request at the police station for them to give him back his beer.

In court he copped to having the bottle in hand, but claimed was for "a friend". Collings said he left it on the theatre's steps not because he was trying to ditch the evidence but he had a bus to catch – somehow he could not carry the beer and run to the bus stop. The Grand licencee George Blair insisted he had not seen Collings in the bar after closing time and definitely hadn't given him the bottle of beer. He wouldn't even admit the bottle contained beer, until the court found a bottle opener and poured him a glass to sample. Blair dodges any penalties but Collings was fined 20 shillings.

A pub also attracts drunk people who do dumb things – like Joseph Ryan. Late on one May night in 1938 he was at the front door asking for a Mr Morgan. There was no-one staying there by that name so the night porter told him to bugger off. Which he did, but only to take a running charge at the glass door, his head swathed in his overcoat. In court, Ryan said he didn't charge the door, he was just knocking on it. "I evidently did smash the door," he said. "I didn't mean to do it." For his drunken destruction Ryan was fined £5.

In 1954 there were plans to make the Grand "the most modern hotel outside the metropolitan area", the *Mercury* reported. This included extending the Burelli Street frontage into a vacant lot next-door, where a lounge and beer garden would be built. A new floor with 30 bedrooms would take the total accommodation to 80. There was even the idea to add in "an American oyster bar" for businessmen's lunches.

By the 1980s, the pub was known as Hal's Tavern, after licencee Hal Browne took over. Browne was a former league player, taking the field as a centre for the Balmain Tigers from 1964 to 1970. In 1969 the Tigers made the grand final against South Sydney, but injury ruled Browne out – though he went down in rugby league folklore by donning the tiger mascot suit that Saturday afternoon. The Tigers won the grand final 11-2.

In the 1990s, the name changed to Cooney's after Kevin Cooney took it over, turning it into an Irish pub where all the bar staff had to learn how to pour a Guinness properly. By 2008 the pub was in the hands of the RDL Group, who also owned a number of other pubs and bars in the city – including the Harp Hotel, The Glasshouse and Castros. The new owners returned The Grand name to the venue and in mid-2009 opened the door on the refurbished hotel that included four bars, a bistro, lounge area, pool room and a nightclub.

A year later, part of the RDL Group ended up in receivership and receivers took over at The Harp and The

Glasshouse, among others. The Grand, owned by one of their other companies, wasn't affected.

In the 2010s, the venue got a black eye by appearing on the NSW government's violent venues list, compiled from the number of violent events that occurred. In 2012-13 it was the only Illawarra nightspot on the statewide list. For the region that was an improvement on 2009, where nine venues made the cut with The Glasshouse ranked in second spot. The Grand was there again in 2017, with 14 assaulted recorded at the venue.

Reaching for the sky

Big changes were happening in Keira Street in the mid-1950s. It has already begun developing a reputation as one of the key streets in the city in terms of business. That reputation was solidified when national companies decided to set up in Keira Street, building multi-storey structures.

"Within a year Keira Street between Crown and Smith streets, will present an entirely new face," the *South Coast Times* wrote in 1954, "comprising two, three and five-storied buildings and modern, gleaming shopfronts."

The first of those was the AMP Building on the south-western corner of Keira and Market streets. "When completed it will be the foremost commercial building in the city," the *Times* wrote of the five-storey building that opened its doors on May 10, 1956.

To mark the opening the *Mercury* ran an eight-page liftout on the building, which suggests it was a bit of a big deal for the city. In fact it was just big, full stop; the

Mercury stated it was "the largest office block in any rural centre in NSW". It also boasted the first passenger lift in a building in Wollongong. Which is hardly surprising, given most buildings in the city were only two-storeys, and why would you need a lift there?

It wasn't the most visually appealing building, a rather blah brown structure taking up a corner block. Though the *Mercury* managed to see the upside of all that blandness.

"The design is functional without any extreme features as these may attract attention for a time but lose appeal and eventually become dated."

Given that photos of the time show the building in black and white, here's a detailed description from the *Mercury* of what it looked it in 1956.

"The main façade is a balance between face brickwork and glass, framed by two wing walls rendered light green and projecting concrete hoods. Shopfronts and supporting columns between show windows are finished in matching teal blue ceramic tiles.

"Wide continuous concrete hoods over windows provide protection from the direct rays of the sun. Green rendered fins provide interesting contrast to the wide expanse of face brick spandrels and the white colour of the hoods."

The Australian Mutual Provident Society (that's what the AMP stand for, by the way) didn't occupy all five floors itself. Instead, it made a no doubt handy sum renting out office space to other business on all floors. These included a typewriter salesman, an optometrist, a hairdresser, an accountant, a solicitor, the Audiophone Company and something called "the Scout Shop".

Diagonally across the road would be a much better example of architecture in the National Mutual building. Built in 1956, it featured four storeys – two across most of the building but adding another two for a clock tower. During construction provision was made to add extra storeys if desired, though that never happened. In fact, the building has remained remarkably unchanged, right down to the small iron fence that still runs along the Market Street frontage. Only the glass top on the clock tower was an addition after construction was completed.

Incidentally, for a time National Mutal later moved across the road and took over naming rights to the AMP Building, thereby confusing later historians – but the building on the north-eastern corner of Keira and Market streets *is* the original National Mutual building.

The third office tower to go up in 1956 was the MLC Building. It was located on Keira Street, next-door to the AMP digs. In an indicator of how new these towers were and how quickly Keira Street was changing, the southern neighbour of the MLC was a used car dealer on what appeared to be a dirt lot. How many new office blocks have to deal with a car dealership for a neighbour?

In terms of blandness, it outdid the AMP Building, even the *Mercury* struggling to dress it up, figuring the best part was the "magnificent panoramic views" from the windows. Meaning the best thing you could do was look *away* from the building.

"The construction is of steel frame encased in

concrete," the *Mercury* wrote. "Floors are of hollow blocks, concrete ribs and slab. All machine-finished floor surfaces are covered with lino tiles." Like the AMP, it too would come with a lift; a necessity in a five-storey building.

Perhaps a sign of the underwhelming nature of the Keira Street building was that pages of a *Mercury* supplement devoted several pages to MLC's buildings in places other than Wollongong. It wrote of the buildings in Sydney – both its existing premises and new ones under construction in North Sydney. Though to be honest, the North Sydney building just looked like a big shoebox.

The Keira Street MLC building also has a footnote as being the location of one of the city's earliest bomb threats. In July 1967, the building was evacuated, workers milling around on the footpath during the lunchtime rush.

Someone had rung the Wollongong Fire Station, saying they had planted a bomb inside. Police rushed to the scene, making their way through the building – which at the time included the local ABC radio station – telling them to get out. A search revealed no sign of a bomb, making it the fourth such hoax threat that year following on from calls about a Port Kembla school, a train and at Piccadilly in upper Crown Street.

A decade later, in July 1964, Colonial Mutual Life opened up its own tower on the strip, on the southwestern corner of Keira and Crown streets. In an ad, the company said the decision to build the six-storey tower in Wollongong was "indicative of the society's faith in the continued development and progress of this city".

It was taller than the MLC or AMP buildings; it reached 100ft (30.4 metres) into the sky. According to the *Mercury*, that was the maximum building height allowed outside of the capital cities.

The ANZ Bank would take up space on the ground floor, and would include this new-fangled invention of airconditioning. Rather than nab the top storey in its own building, the CML took the second level. Maybe they didn't want the workers distracted by the views of the water and escarpment out the window, which at 100-feet high would have been unavailable from any other building in the city.

Wonderwalls

A French-Canadian model has kept watch over Keira Street since 2012 – but she's not alive. She's a creation of Melbourne Street artist Rone (it's short for Tyrone). He painted Celestine on the southern wall of the Dion Building near the Smith Street intersection as part of the regular Wonderwalls festival.

"It sounded more interesting than painting another wall in Fitzroy," the Melbourne-based Rone said. "I love the idea of doing something for the community that's appreciated and of being able to paint alongside some great artists."

It is one of four murals that have adorned walls along this stretch of Keira Street, though you have to hunt for one of them, and another has disappeared altogether. Sam Clouston painted the Asian supermarket wall facing Celestine while on the other side of the supermarket is a collaboration from artists Shida and Adnate. That second one is hard to see because, since it was painted, the small gap between the supermarket and Debutante was filled in by a very skinny building. To get a look you have to peer over a metal fence and view it on a very sharp angle.

The fourth, by Brisbane-born graffiti artist Sofles has gone altogether. That was on the northern wall of Debutante and is now completely covered up by that very skinny building.

Those four are part of a street art festival that started in 2012 when graphic design and events business Verb Syndicate and artists' group The Hours decided it would raise the appreciation for street art.

"The aim of the festival is ultimately to shine a positive light on the work done with aerosols," Verb Syndicate's Simon Grant said.

"We want people who are interested in these art forms to see Wollongong as a place that can cut it with the rest of the world. Bigger projects like these are being done throughout Europe and America and we're catching up pretty quick here with this festival."

It would later move to beautifying walls in Port Kembla and become a tourist attraction for fans of street art. There's no doubt the works in the Keira Street and elsewhere in the Wollongong CBD have played a part in the creation of a new vibe and feel in the city. Along with the hip small bars and wide range of restaurants, the brightly coloured walls have livened up the city.

"It's amazing how artwork can completely change how people look at a space," said artist Georgia Hill, who painted a mural at 281 Keira Street and a joint effort at Wollongong train station. "It makes people walk through their town a different way, and value the space themselves.

"Like anything, if you show it a bit of love and attention, it can turn into something else completely."

A football visionary

While this book largely confines itself to that section of Keira Street between Smith and Burelli streets, allowances have been made for events and locations that happened outside those boundaries as long as you could see them from Keira Street.

For this story I'm going to stretch that rule a bit, but it's for a story that is just too good to leave out. It concerns Country Rugby League chairman Dudley Locke. If you stood on the northeastern corner of Keira and Burelli streets in the 1950s and looked towards where the multi-storey car park is now, you might just have been able to see the Lockes' house at 246 Keira Street (it would have been within the footprint of the car park). It was likely when Locke was sitting at home one night in 1953 that he came up with a most audacious scheme – to poach eight players from the Sydney league clubs, including Clive Churchill. Yes, that Clive Churchill, the future Immortal.

The plan was bankrolled by the large funds from the

Illawarra Leagues Club, which had officially opened in 1951. Two years later, in part because of the large amounts of beer being sold at the club (it went from 74 gallons a week when the club opened to 720 gallons in 1953), Locke had enough ready cash to spend £12,500 on buying players. He refuted the suggestion that the club was "angling" to get an Illawarra team into the Sydney competition. "That's ridiculous," Locke said. "We will make our competition so strong down here that Sydney clubs will want to play in it."

On June 10, 1953, a touring US team played a country side at Wollongong Showground. The match saw an influx of Australian players, where the leagues club started secret negotiations with some of them. Once word got out that the club was waving around lucrative contracts there was interest from a lot of players, the *Sydney Morning Herald* reported.

By this stage, the media had linked one very big player to the Illawarra Leagues Club bid – Kangaroo captain and South Sydney player Clive Churchill. The gossip was that he had already signed a five-year deal to play in Wollongong from 1954. Both Locke and Churchill tried to scotch the rumours. "There has been talk of my transferring there," Churchill told the Sydney press, "but my home is here and I would not do anything before seeing South Sydney."

A few days later, Locke let the cat out of the bag while announcing he had signed Country winger Jack Lumsden and Kangaroo centre Harry Wells. "The Illawarra club is trying to engage a number of topline players," he said.

"We are trying to form a strong competition here. We have made overtures to other players, including Clive Churchill, but as yet only two have been signed."

That was enough to put the wind up South Sydney, who went to a meeting of the NSW League and tabled a motion specifically designed to halt Locke's plan. The club wanted to see all players in the Kangaroo team soon to tour New Zealand bound to their present club for the next season. Which would obviously mean Souths would get to keep Churchill. It was narrowly defeated 18-14.

On the weekend of June 20, Churchill travelled down to Wollongong to sign a £2500 contract that would see him play in the Illawarra league for five seasons; the leagues club also committed to finding him a house and a job. "An offer like mine was too good to reject," Churchill said. "Sydney clubs could not give me anything like the terms, so when I saw that there was good accommodation and a steady job I snapped up the offer."

Among the other players who took advantage of the leagues club's cash splash were Noel Pidding, Brian Carlson, Brian Orrock and Churchill's Souths team-mate Les Cowie. In Sydney, footy teams decided there was some merit in this unique funding model and decided to set up their own leagues clubs.

"Most Sydney clubs realise that the only counter to the Wollongong plan is cash," the *Sunday Mail* reported, "and that it can be made in large enough amounts only by clubs along the Illawarra lines.

"St George has already established its 'social club'. Canterbury-Bankstown will have one going before next season. South Sydney and Manly-Warringah have ideas, and this week a supporter offered North Sydney £1000 to get its club started. If they get enough liquor licences they'll be right."

When the Illawarra Leagues Club allocated the players to various clubs in the Wollongong competition; Christian Brothers (now Collegians) got the prize of Churchill for the 1954 season. The leagues club also offloaded to the clubs the responsibility of fulfilling the promise of a house and a job for each player. The clubs had 60 days to take care of that, otherwise the leagues club would step in and reallocate the players.

But The Little Master was getting cold feet; he found the flat he had been promised was in disrepair and the top-notch role he was supposed to have at the leagues club was behind the bar. But perhaps top of Churchill's mind was that his wife was unhappy about leaving the big smoke. "I signed the contract with the Illawarra Leagues Club in haste," he told the *Sydney Morning Herald*, "and I now regret it. My wife does not want to go to Wollongong."

He was interested in becoming a publican; so Souths aimed to woo him back with the help of supporters willing to help him achieve that goal. "My present plans are to play in Wollongong next year," said Churchill, muddying the waters, "but I also have the chance of moving into the hotel business.

"Should this happen I may retire from football until the business is well-established. This does not mean that I am contemplating retiring from football forever."

Not surprisingly, Locke was most unimpressed. "Churchill is bound to play in Wollongong for the next five years," he said. "He has signed a £2500 contract and has agreed to work at the Illawarra Social Club. We will not release him from his contract." He added he would make sure the Souths player did not play anywhere else for the five-year length of the contract.

The NSW League stepped in to help Souths and Churchill by stating that, as the Illawarra Leagues Club wasn't affiliated with the Sydney body that it would not recognise the contract Locke had devised. Rather conveniently, at the very same meeting, Souths tabled Churchill's freshly-signed contract for registration. Churchill's Souths team-mate Cowie also wanted out of his Wollongong contract.

Locke said he wasn't too concerned with what Cowie did; it was Churchill's reneging and the precedent it was setting he was unhappy with. "We are not in the least concerned about what the NSW Rugby League does in this matter," he said. "Its attitude is consistent with the attitude of all district clubs in Sydney. For years they have pilfered the greatest players the country has had. Clive Churchill is an example.

"We are trying to restore country football to its former strength. But now the League has said Churchill will not play here many of the other players we have signed up are not keen to join us. Churchill is the backbone of the team we are building."

The player regretted what he had done but felt he had made the right move for himself. "I feel sure Wollongong would have released me from the contract if I had explained," he said, and then walked back his complaint of being offered dud employment. "Wollongong was giving me a good job in the leagues club, but I now find I am doing better in Sydney."

In October 1953, he sought permission to speak to the leagues club at its next meeting – and then didn't show. Churchill decided a Thursday night meeting wasn't convenient – which really sounds like the actions of a man not keen to face the music. So his lawyer had to deliver the bad news that Churchill believed the contract he signed with the Illawarra Leagues Club wasn't binding, and he owed it to rugby league to stay with Souths. Oh yeah, and he didn't like the job the club found him either – even though he had days earlier called it a "good job".

"My client also desires that I point out to you that, with respect to the position offered to him," the lawyer said "it would appear that the position offered to my client would entail him working in an unregistered club where the law so far as the Gaming and Betting Act is concerned is constantly broken and, of course, should the police at any time in the future take action, then his security of employment would be greatly jeopardised."

Locke said that was crap; the club had a liquor licence and no gambling was allowed. He was very unimpressed with Churchill indeed – in fact most of the city was. "This joker has captained Australia for 40 matches – an all-time record – and when a chap like that wallows in the dirt something should be done," Locke told the meeting.

"You can be quite sure that had this club fallen down

on its side of the contract, there was no doubt what Churchill would have done. I am quite sure he would have demanded and sued us for the £2500 and for the £15 per week guaranteed wage for five years."

So that's the same course of action the leagues club took; they engaged the services of a QC and prepared to drag Churchill through the courts. "Churchill's arrogant attitude has decided us on this action," Locke told the media.

The plan was to restrain him from playing elsewhere and consider claiming damages. There was no expectation that this would be a quick fix; Locke wasn't expecting to see the court case start for months. While waiting for his day in court, Locke continued waving money around to drag elite players to the Illawarra.

One of those was Puig Aubert, the best French league player of all time. And perhaps one of the most unusual; the fullback was reputed to have taken a cigarette on the field several times, once catching a ball with one hand because he held a ciggie in the other. Locke offered the Frenchman £14,000, which included a £6250 sign-on fee, £500 per year as a playing bonus and a job with a guaranteed weekly wage of £20.

Locke was also thinking outside the league square, looking to bring top-class soccer player Stanley Matthews over to play his sport locally. He got the same offer as Aubert. NSW Soccer Football Association director JC Cobb thought it a good idea but not enough to entice Matthews to the South Coast. And anyway, it would be better to spread that money around the players already here. "I would like to see a number of such players put on a full-time or part-time coaching basis and told to concentrate on the schoolboys and the junior players," Cobb said. "If this is done, the full effects will not be seen for perhaps five years, but the results will be well worthwhile, even spectacular."

In the end neither sportsman took Locke up on his offer. Meanwhile, the grand scheme to buy a player for each local league team had well and truly come unstuck. Churchill and Cowie had already left, while Ken McCaffrey wasn't keen to play with Western Suburbs and Port Kembla didn't want their allocated player Brian Carlson.

Meanwhile, up in Sydney, Churchill had pulled on the Souths jersey for a few trial matches ahead of the 1954 season; making it perfectly clear he wasn't going to honour his Illawarra contract. After Churchill finally came down to face the committee in March, the leagues club agreed to let both he and Cowie out of their contracts.

Churchill admitted he should have spoken to the club much, much earlier. But, like so many footballers who would come after him, Churchill recognised his time in the game was short and he had to make hay (ie cash) while the sun was shining.

"I am now recognised as one of Australia's leading footballers, but I have seen some of the world's best today, become a has-been tomorrow – forgotten by those who came to cheer – and left entirely to their own resources," he told the committee. "I hope to play representative football for many years yet but I have an obligation to myself and my family to ensure that when I am forgotten I will have something."

There was no word on whether the leagues club got something in return for stepping aside. Though Locke's efforts did have the effect of creating a resurgence of interest in the local league as people began to pack the grandstands to watch the games.

A place for teenagers

In 1968 a "way out" place opened up on Keira Street, right on the southern side of the Victoria Street intersection. A coffee lounge, it included pinball machines, pool tables and "a psychedelic cellar" where people could watch TV.

The description of "way out" came from Reverend Noel Hart, so take it with a grain of salt. The building was The Crossways drop-in centre, started by the Anglican Church. Coincidentally, it sat on the very same block that was home to the Salvation Army's citadel in the early 1900s.

"The building we have secured is ideal," Rev Hart told the *Mercury*. "It looks a little way-out and is certainly a different style of building to those nearby."

The Crossways was aimed squarely at teenagers, with the Rev Hart hoping to save a few souls from descending into some really nasty stuff. No, not drugs – breaking stuff.

"We want to reach these young people before they get into trouble and before they reach the vandalism stage," Rev Hart said. "The centre will simply be a place where they can drop in for a chat with friends. I feel there are hundreds of kids in Wollongong who would make use of such a centre."

The centre officially opened its doors on July 9, after high school students from Smiths Hill and Keira Boys had volunteered to paint the walls – which included those psychedelic flower murals in the cellar. A month later the *Mercury* reported the place was a hotspot for teenagers, though a photo of Rev Hart looking bored while drinking a cappuccino (oddly served in a teacup) with two teenage girls didn't make the place seem happening.

Those two teens – Rebecca Crane and Diane Smith were there because they liked the reverend. "And because it's relaxed, like someone else's living room," they said. "And there's no pressure on you to keep on buying cups of coffee like there is in any other coffee bar."

Despite the pool tables and pinballs, it seemed that sitting down and chatting was the most popular pastime. And what they were chatting about was sex. "In fact, it's our favourite subject," Rev Hart said, not at all creepily. "These kids want to bring this out into the open."

Open daily from 10am to 11pm, with teenagers hanging around not buying coffees, the costs at Crossways started mounting. Operating costs were estimated at $130 a week and then there were plans to buy amplifiers and a projector, which was another $3000. While the Anglican church was able to tap benefactors for a while, their aim for Crossways was that it would be paying its own way six months after opening. But it never reached that target. Those benefactors kept contributing beyond that six-month period but soon started dropping off.

By 1970, the teenagers using the centre ended up working to raise the money to keep it afloat. They staged a walkathon from Kiama to Wollongong, which raised $1000. Rev Hart's replacement Graham Frizzell couldn't bear the thought of closing the doors, having seen a side of the city of which many were ignorant.

"He knows all about the broken homes, the runaway fathers and the mothers with a drink problem," the *Mercury* reported. "He is a confidante for kids who don't take their problems home because there is no-one there or no-one interested enough to listen."

Little Richard

At first the Illawarra wasn't too keen on this strange new beast known as rock and roll. In October 1956, the city's first "rock and roll" dance – held at the Corrimal Community Centre – made the front page of the *Illawarra Mercury*. It wasn't to mark the first event of its kind, but to note the heavy presence of police outside the venue.

Four cops in uniform were stationed outside, with more plainclothes police inside, fooling no-one. They were there to stop the kids from going crazy after being whipped into a frenzy. But no rioting occurred – there weren't enough people inside for that. As many as 20 people milled outside along with those uniformed police, but none dared go inside.

"The dance was scheduled to start at 8pm, but by 9.30pm only four couples were on the lonely floor," the paper reported. "And only one couple was 'hepping' it up. The rest of the dancers were dancing in a conventional manner." None of the dancers were undercover cops, by the way.

Keira Street

The police had a theory for the low attendance; the mums wouldn't let their kids go after hearing of the wild behaviour in London a month earlier at screenings of the Bill Haley movie *Rock Around the Clock*.

Almost a year later, the city seemed to have made its peace with this music the young folk loved. Little Richard was on a tour of Australia. It was one of the first rock tours of this country, and the first to reach Wollongong.

Bringing along the likes of Johnny O'Keefe and Eddie Cochrane, Little Richard kicked off the tour with a gig at the Crown Theatre, then on Keira Street, opposite what is now the Grand Hotel. The local paper again gave the concert the front-page treatment, but this time there was no mention of the cops. O'Keefe and his band the Dee Jays started the show "with a twang of electric guitars and a clash of cymbals".

"The Australian group, with its wailing saxophones, provided the 'shocker' of the night, sung by Johnny O'Keefe," the reporter wrote. "O'Keefe swaying in all directions, sung a number, *Flip, Flop and Fly*, which is a current hit in America. He finished on his knees wrestling with the microphone. The audience screamed and stamped their feet while O'Keefe sang." O'Keefe biographer Jeff Apter paints a different story of the Wild One's Wollongong show. Apter writes that the crowd was booing O'Keefe, calling for the American headliner instead. No shrinking violet, O'Keefe called on his band to stop, and then gave the rowdy crowd a response that has gone down in history. "You may boo me and you may throw things at me. But you all pay your money to see me

– because you love me!".

According to the *Mercury*, Cochran's performance "put the audience into full swing", followed by "the female Elvis Presley" in one-hit wonder Alis Lesley. "She squealed instead of grunting, as Presley does, after each line," the *Mercury* noted.

As would be the case for every rock and roll show from here on, the headliner got the most attention. "His version of *Tutti Frutti* and *Lucille* were met with tremendous applause and he could be barely heard above the screaming and stomping of feet," the front page of the *Mercury* read. "Besides being an expert showman, Little Richard also appeared to be an expert gymnast."

The *Mercury* interviewed Little Richard in his hotel room after the show, where he revealed his desire to turn to God. The performer – who had thrown religious booklets into the teenaged crowd – told the reporter this music caper was only temporary. "Rock 'n' roll to me is a living. Everyone has to have a living," he said. "But my real ambition is to become a minister." That came sooner than expected – when the tour reached Newcastle, Little Richard famously chose to forsake rock and roll for the Lord, throwing his jewels into the Hunter River.

The show had an effect on Wollongong teens, and local bands started to form. According to music historian Warren Wheeler, the first may have been Johnny Johnson and the Rebels. Forming in late 1957, the band played venues like the Patch, The Rex at Thirroul and Fairy Meadow's Charles Hotel. They even travelled to Victoria to record an album's worth of tunes, though apparently no copies have survived.

To the likely befuddlement of parents, rock and roll was still around when the 1960s arrived. In 1960 American singer Crash Craddock toured Australia. He hadn't set the charts on fire in his own country, but Australians went crazy for him. On February 2, he played two shows at the Crown Theatre and drew in around 4000 fans across both shows. The *Mercury*'s coverage of the show paints a wild scene, with fans waiting outside rushing every taxi that pulled up in case a rock star was about to climb out.

Things were also frenetic inside. "Teenage girls swarmed around the foot of the stage," the *Mercury* reported, "when the star of the performance, Crash Craddock, began to sing the final number at the end of the second session. As Craddock came off, a burly bodyguard and offsider threw themselves around the star and tucked his head under their arms to get him through the throng of screaming girls milling around the stage."

Wollongong Central

It took longer than expected, had stops and starts and even changed its name but the multi-storey Wollongong Central shopping centre finally opened for business in October 2014.

That was almost a decade after the city got the first sniff of something happening. In 2006 Wollongong Central owner GPT told Franklins supermarket it would not be renewing its lease in the shopping centre – which was only on the eastern side of Keira Street at the time. A GPT spokesperson said the supermarket had to go because it wasn't part of the group's plans to redevelop the centre, which included building on the western side of the street.

Around the same time, plans were revealed for the building across the road – then tagged GPT West Keira – after the rumours had been swirling for the past year. It would include shopping, commercial and residential space. The two centres would be linked by a pedestrian tunnel and a two-level walkway and road bridge joining the car parks. Some of the land on the proposed site was owned by the council, who agreed to sell the lots to GPT, but baulked at selling off Crown Lane, which the group had planned to close.

A year later the formal plans were lodged with the state government for approval, and they looked a little different to what is there now. As well as that road bridge, there was also an eight-screen cinema complex that would go into the eastern end of the existing Wollongong Central. On top of the new GPT West Keira structure would be an 18-storey residential tower and a 10-storey commercial building, both to be developed at a later stage.

Aside from the need to get planning approval, there was something else that stood in the way – Bing Lee. The retailer occupied the store at 202 Keira Street that previously housed the likes of Anthony Hordern's, Waltons and Norman Ross. And they had a long-term lease on the site and no intentions of packing up and moving. It stayed put even after the May 2008 construction approval from the government.

The other businesses along the western side between Market and Crown streets had moved out by this stage. "We still have a long-term lease," Bing Lee property manager Ben Nursoo said. "GPT are going ahead and we are the only people still trading."

And then GPT wasn't going ahead. In September 2008, the group announced it was putting the project on hold for two years due to the global financial crisis.

"We are extremely positive about the region and the market here," said GPT head of retail Mark Fookes, "but the deterioration in the global investment market has had an impact on … the risk and return profile and put us in this position."

Instead, the group would limit itself to redeveloping the existing Wollongong Central at that point in time. It was bad news for those business owners around Bing Lee who had already had to pack up and move. One of whom was McAndrew's Florist Sonja Daly, who moved west along Crown Street. "I'm happy that we're here now, but I feel like saying 'sucked in' to them," she said. Mylan restaurant had moved across the road, while Bing Lee could now stay put until at least 2010.

It was also bad news for the city, who saw GPT's big plans as a vote of confidence in Wollongong and felt other business would flow in on the back of that. "We looked at this as a catalyst for kick-starting the CBD," said Australian Property Council's Illawarra branch chair Geoff Jones. It also stymied the council's plans to upgrade the mall – it had earmarked the $3.6 million in developer funds from West Keira to be used to upgrade the strip.

The city breathed a sigh of relief in mid-2011 when GPT said the West Keira development was back on. Though that would also mean Bing Lee would get its marching orders, given that long-term lease had expired in the interim.

There were some changes – that road bridge and cinema complex got the chop (despite the city being chronically underserved by modern cinemas) and retail floor space dropped from 20,000sqm to 18,000sqm. And people could forget about seeing Big W or Kmart in the centre. "For us it was about prioritising what we can do to create a CBD experience," said GPT development manager Steven Turner. "We wanted to present a greater variety of shops and with a discount department store, we couldn't have done that."

Turner said the revised plans lodged with the government should be seen as proof GPT were serious with Wollongong. "This application reflects our ability to get this to the market as soon as we possibly can. We're excited to bring what we believe is a truly unique and iconic CBD retail experience to Wollongong."

Work started on the site just before Christmas 2011 with GPT tipping the $200 million complex would be open by early 2014. They missed that target by about six months, in part because they discovered the rock underneath the site was much harder than expected. Excavating the site took longer – and was louder – than expected. Also, when in the home straight and creating the tunnel under Keira Street and the alfresco dining strip along the western side, several weeks of heavy rain caused even more delays. That latter wrinkle was a pain for businesses along that stretch, because fencing had gone up along the closed Keira Street, making it uninviting for pedestrians to navigate their way through to a restaurant.

On October 9, 2014, it was all over and the doors were opened. After almost a decade, the locals were champing at the bit to get inside; stores were packed and the queues were five deep at the upstairs food court. It's unclear how many people noticed the quirky touches on the bottom floor – 3000 steel colanders on the ceiling and 5000 rolling pins covering the columns. Not everyone was there for the big day; Guzman y Gomez, Max Brenner and Coco Cubano were among the 10 tenants not yet ready to open. Ten years later, of those three, only Guzman would still be there; in that time several businesses cycled through the Keira-Crown corner spot first occupied by Max Brenner.

Given the big crowds, the block of Keira Street had remained closed on the day, bands, rides and speeches taking place on the bitumen. The Illawarra Property Council held a lunch on the day, where the centre opening – by now referred to as Wollongong Central rather than West Keira – had made the panelists were giddy with the feeling of possibility for the next decade.

"I think Wollongong will be surprised itself with where it heads up – even given what it's aiming at now," Turner said. Susanne Pini, an architect who worked on the Wollongong Central development, said she and her husband had bought a unit in the city 20 years ago and held onto it because they felt something might happen here.

"Wollongong is always in our minds as being on the cusp of greatness," she said. "In 10 years we won't be on the cusp any more – we will be there."

A royal visit

On Thursday, February 11, 1954 the section of Keira Street between Smith and Burelli streets was closed to traffic. And it wasn't the only street either; Burelli and Smith were closed, as was Crown Street and Church Street.

The reason was because the city had a special visitor – the Queen was coming to town. The Queen had a whistle-stop tour of the city on February 11 – she arrived in the morning, drove through the streets to the city centre where she made a speech. Then she hopped on a train at Bulli in the afternoon and was gone.

Along Keira Street, as on the other streets on the Queen's route, shops and houses were decked out with flags, bunting and decorations.

"It is estimated that firms have spent thousands of pounds in decorations," the *Mercury* said. "Shop windows have been dressed in royal tonings, Crowns surmount buildings, Union Jacks and Australian flags flutter at an average of one to every 20 yards of building frontage.

"Royal motifs decorate street corners; and everywhere cars have been decorated with coloured streamers and flags. Stores report that they have never before experienced such a rush in the sale of decorations and flags."

On Crown Street, right on the Keira Street intersection, an arch was constructed with workmen still busy painting and decorating it in the last days before the arrival of her Royal Highness.

One man was unimpressed with some of the preparations. John Waters wrote to the *Mercury* outraged the mayor planned chocolate wheels "and similar games of chance". "I am sure that a large proportion of the citizens would, like myself, find this proposal most repugnant," wowser Waters wrote.

On the day all traffic in the city would stop at 11.45am. The Royal party would drive down Crown Street, turn left into Keira and hang a right into Smith Street to loop back to the town hall to deliver an address. Then she'd head up Crown Street, left into Keira and left into Burelli and then into Church Street for a luncheon. Once that was over she'd go to the showground, do a few laps for the crowd and then drive through North Wollongong on her way to Bulli.

Once at Bulli, she would do the opposite of most commuters to Sydney and figure a train was a better option than a car. The reasoning was "because it would be imposing too much strain on the Queen to expect her to drive back to Sydney by car," the *Mercury* reported.

The sudden decision to take the train would be good

news for the staff at Bulli station. It meant they'd see the Queen, though they did have to put up a lot of last-minute Union Jacks. "We have been flat-out and haven't had time to breathe," station master Jack Henson said the day before she arrived.

Back in the city, in preparation for the visit barriers were erected along the side of the road at Keira Street and elsewhere. Motorists were also advised not to park next to the barrier as any cars still there on the day of the visit would be towed. If they needed a parking space, Beaton Park would be open for the public coming in to see the Queen.

Those barriers had been trucked down from Newcastle after the Queen's visit on the Tuesday. They only arrived in Wollongong on the Wednesday afternoon and police cadets and probationary constables had just 24 hours to set up seven kilometres of barriers. Then, on the Thursday afternoon, they'd have to be taken down just as quickly so the barriers could be sent to Canberra to prepare for the Queen's visit to the nation's capital.

Areas of the Keira Street footpath between Crown and Burelli streets were set aside for special groups. The Girl Guides and the Boy Scouts were able to sit in front of the barriers on the western side, with pensioners given exclusive access to the eastern side.

The Scouts, Guides, pensioners and everyone else were told to stay behind the barriers at all times. "Chaos could easily be the result of members of the public climbing through barriers and crowding onto roadways once the procession has passed," a police officer told the

South Coast Times.

Town Clerk WH Mitchell also encouraged the citizens to behave themselves in front of the Queen. "We should give our Queen a right Royal welcome and show her that Wollongong is loyal and patriotic," he said. "Cheer to your hearts content without making foolish comments which might be embarrassing. Welcome her with your whole heart, but make things as easy as possible for her so that her memories of Wollongong will be pleasant.

"It is our first opportunity of welcoming a reigning monarch and we have exceeded anything that has been done in the past."

On the following day police Inspector Magnay, who was in charge of co-ordinating the officers during the visit, said he was happy with how the citizens carried themselves. "The huge crowds were exceptionally well-behaved and I personally compliment them on their demure, which was a credit to this district of ours," Inspector Magnay said.

It seems even the crims were interested in the Royal visit; during the time the Queen and Prince Philip were in town there was not a single arrest. There was only one arrest on the whole day, and that was an incident of illegal gambling after the Royals left town.

Despite what the Inspector said, there were some incidents of poor behaviour. After the Royal luncheon at the Soldiers Memorial Hall, the doors were opened so people could have a look. As soon as they got in, people started snaffling the flowers and other decorations as souvenirs.

Keira Street

"The selfishness of some people and their destructiveness was soon realised and the hall was again promptly cleared and closed," the *South Coast Times* reported. Fortunately someone had seen fit to remove the plates and cutlery, placing them under police guard before the hordes rushed in.

Boxing

The idea of someone erecting a stadium in Keira Street in 1915 so as to stage boxing matches didn't sit well with some city aldermen. Which was a little odd given there were already bouts going on at the Star and Globe Theatres – on Church Street and the corner of Church Street and Globe Lane respectively. To make matters confusing for a modern researcher, the ads and stories about boxing events say they were taking place at the "Globe Stadium" or the "Star Stadium", though I'd reckon it's safe to assume they are the theatres under a different name.

Just where in Keira Street this stadium was is a little unclear. If we use the theatre/stadium double act, it could be at the Crown Theatre at the eastern Keira-Burelli corner. Or it could be just to the north, tucked in behind O'Brien's Hotel – the pub also known as the Settlers Arms and then the Royal Albert. In the 1910s, there were a number of stories about visiting fighters training at O'Brien's Hotel (with times that the public could turn up and watch). One would assume the fighter wasn't training in a bar but some sort of boxing ring, which makes it seem likely that was the "stadium" the aldermen were so angry about.

At any rate, it seems what the aldermen were discussing was a request to build a fence around the building. The building itself had already been approved by the council; some aldermen were surprised to hear that, making one question whether they were even awake during council meetings.

Several reverends in the city sent a petition to the council outraged about the possibility of boxing taking place in Keira Street - perhaps because they lived nearby. There were calls that the council endorse the petition. Alderman Lance agreed with that idea wholeheartedly and felt the reverends shouldn't have to put up with "a lot of boisterous noises".

"Why don't these chaps who go in for boxing go to the front, where they ought to be, instead of bashing each other about? Lance asked rhetorically. "It was shameful to think that the council were countenancing such a disgraceful procedure."

Alderman Marks was also a fan of sending boxing fans off to fight in the war. "If they wanted to give a high moral tone to the town," the *Mercury* reported Marks as saying, "it was necessary to stop this sort of thing. It was demoralising and they as aldermen should not allow it. By granting permission to boxing shows they were hindering enlistment."

Jumping onto that bandwagon was Alderman Sutton.

"We had about 300 young fellows of eligible age to go to the front and yet the response had been practically nil," he said.

Other aldermen at the meeting pointed out that wrestling had been going on in the Keira Street venue for a year but none of his colleagues had complained about that. Others said the building had already been approved so whingeing about it now was a bit late (or words to that effect). In the end the effort to adopt the reverends' petition failed.

Though it isn't clear whether any boxing ever happened there. The opening night was to be August 28, 1915, where Wollongong's Billy Brodie would take on Tony Ross from Coledale over 20 rounds. But that fight – and the opening night – didn't take place. It was called off for unknown reasons, the Brodie-Ross bout moved to the Globe on September 25. For the record, Ross was out of his depth. He only landed one punch on Brodie, who knocked him out in the second round with a left to the jaw.

The best buses

If you wait around on Keira Street long enough, you'll see a Dion's bus. The family-run bus company has been a regular on the street, since the first bus carried passengers back in 1923. Some of the family members have become a little too familiar with Keira Street; in 1927 nine-year-old Ernie Dion landed on the road after being hit by a car near the Market Street intersection. He ended up in hospital with a fractured arm and leg.

The family arrived in Wollongong in 1907, after Thomas Chong had entered Australia in 1880, later bringing wife Annie to Australia from China. The family surname that is emblazoned on the side of the buses evolved over time; the first child, Ivy was given the surname of Chong Da On. The second, Tom, was Chong Di On, and it continued until Edward was born in 1908, and the "Chong" was dropped and his surname was Di-On. Over time, the hyphen disappeared and the family name became Dion by 1912.

The family had set up a market garden in Fairy

Meadow when they arrived. But when Thomas passed away in 1920, leaving Annie and their 12 children (and one on the way), the need to diversify beyond the market garden was obvious.

In February 1923, eldest son Tom opened up a general store on the southwestern corner of Keira and Smith streets, renting out the space next door. It was the start of the Dions' Keira Street property portfolio; in time they would buy some of the buildings adjoining that shop, as well as building on the opposite corner.

In December of that same year, Tom also drove the first Dion's bus – from Wollongong to Balgownie and Bellambi. The well-known Wollongong-Austinmer run began in 1926, with Tom passing on the Balgownie and Bellambi runs to 18-year-old brother Ted.

The city came to feel a fondness for the Dion's No1 bus – which is an unusual thing to feel for a bus company. But it stemmed from the family's Depression-era policy of not refusing rides to those who couldn't afford the fare. Also, if they saw someone running to get to the bus stop, they'd wait for them before driving off.

It was a practice that, while it was a winner with the community, it antagonised the bus inspectors because it meant they so often did not stick to the timetable.

Over the following decades, various Dion family members would appear in court and be fined for timetable breaches. Not that it caused them to mend their ways; breaches were still happening as recently as the mid-1980s when Barney Dion ended up on *A Current Affair* over his battles with the Transport Department.

But the public didn't care; they still backed the family.

Running late wasn't the only reason a Dion would have to front up to court. In the first few decades of the Dion's bus service, there were a lot of rivals and a lot of dodgy tactics. It was commonplace to hear of the bus from one company driving slowly along the route in front of a competitor so as to sweep up all their passengers.

Another tactic saw one bus park alongside another, close enough to block their doors from opening and stopping them picking up fares. And it wasn't unheard of to send a non-timetabled bus out on the road to snatch a rival's customers.

Sometimes the battle between rivals seemed especially personal, as was the case when it came to the bus company owned by the Rowles family. From the 1920s to the 1940s, there were numerous newspaper reports of the tensions between the Rowles and the Dion families.

In May 1928, Tom Dion and Michael Rowles faced court where each alleged the other wanted to fight them.

Rowles – a bus driver for the family firm – claimed Dion came up to him on the street and said he'd heard Rowles wanted to fight him. Rowles said no, to which he claimed Dion said "all right, I will get you on the road some night".

Dion claimed Rowles was the problem; slandering him around town and even using the racial epithet "yellow". He admitted confronting Rowles in the street, but only to settle the matter face-to-face.

"What is your game, spinning tales about me and running me down?" Dion told the court he said to

Rowles. "You will have to cut it out or come round the back and settle it."

However, Dion said he didn't mean a fight, he just wanted to go down a back street to have a chat with Rowles. The judge figured he couldn't charge one and not the other, so both were fined.

In November that same year the two bus rivals were back in court, with Dion accused of throwing rocks at a Rowles bus, and Dion in turn alleging he was assaulted by Michael Rowles.

Michael said he was collecting fares on a bus driven by his brother. When they stopped at Thirroul after dropping off their last passengers, Dion and two others jumped out of a bus across the road. "Now, you blokes, we've got you,' he alleged Dion said. "We will bash your brains out."

Rowles told his brother to floor it and, as the bus drove away, he claimed Dion picked up stones from the road and threw them at the bus. The rear window was shattered and another hit the roof.

In what may have suggested a source for the tensions, Rowles admitted in court the family had applied for the Dion bus route previously and may do so again if Tom Dion was convicted.

Dion admitted there was "unpleasantness" between the two families but he claimed on that night he was just walking across the road to see if there were any passengers waiting for him.

He claimed Rowles said "take this, you yellow bastard" and then kicked him in the stomach. "I fell down and he jumped out and kicked me again."

Both parties called witnesses that supported their side of the story, which made it tricky for the judge. In the end, he dismissed Dion's claim of assault, and Rowles' claim of malicious damage but, oddly upheld the complaint about stone throwing. Dion later appealed the stone-throwing decision but was unsuccessful.

In March 1931, Dion appeared on the margins of another allegation of assault by a member of the Rowles family.

This time, Dion's bus driver Ernest Parkes claimed he was standing on the roadside with another man at North Wollongong when Reuben Rowles pulled up on a motorbike and asked "Which one of you bastards wants a piece of me?".

"A Rowles bus then came along and pulled up," the *Mercury* court report stated. "Six persons, including Mr, Mrs, Miss and Don Rowles got out and defendant then started punching [Parkes], who received about six heavy blows."

A another witness alleged he'd heard Mrs Rowles call out "go on, knock their heads off". When another Dion's bus came along, the Rowles family left.

In his defence, Rueben Rowles claimed Parkes had called him over and then grabbed the bike. When he saw a Rowles bus come along, he called for help.

"I was not going to tackle two of them – I didn't want a hiding," Reuben told the court. "I wouldn't be averse to giving any of Dion's men a hiding if they picked on me."

The magistrate claimed it was a very unusual case and

dismissed it without charging anyone.

In November 1931 Edward Dion claimed he was on the receiving end of stone-throwing, by one Reuben Rowles.

Donald Rowles overtook Dion in a bus leaving Balgownie, followed by Reuben on a motorbike. Ed Dion said he drove on and saw the bus and bike pulled over to the side of the road. As he passed, Dion claimed Reuben stepped out from in front of the parked bus and threw a stone, smashing the windscreen. Reuben said he had not been on a motorbike that night and threw no stones at a Dion bus.

The magistrate dismissed all charges, which prompted Dion's lawyer to note Dion had requested he objected to the magistrate hearing the case as he was biased towards the Rowles family. He said he had dissuaded Dion from that course of action but, after hearing the verdict, decided his client was right.

While that case was unwinding, Don Rowles was in court for running into a Dion bus in Keira Street. Constable Russell testified that he had seen marks on the Rowles bus and asked if he had hit the Dion's bus – to which Don said yes.

Several witnesses testified they had seen the Rowles bus driving at speed down Keira Street from Crown Street, colliding with Ed Dion's bus, which was reversing into its parking area outside the Grand Cinema. Despite the evidence of witnesses and police, the judge claimed to have doubt and dismissed the case.

In 1936, the Dion family finally had a win over the

Rowles, when Ed Dion sued for damage after a Rowles bus sideswiped one of their own. Albert Rowles, who was driving the bus, claimed it was Dion who had weaved across the road and hit him. The judge didn't buy it, awarding Dion £13 in damages.

The climax to the Dion-Rowles rumbles happened in 1944 when Albert Rowles again hit a Dion's bus, this time at Corrimal. Albert ended up in court charged with drink-driving, failing to report an accident and driving in a dangerous manner.

The court heard that, when Rowles turned up to report the accident to police the following day, his words didn't help him. In court, Constable Kiernan said Rowles told him he had driven on to Towradgi and then stopped. After that, Rowles seemed to have blacked out.

"The next thing I knew I found myself sitting on a seat in Marine Parade, Wollongong. That was about 10.30pm and I don't know how I got there," the constable claimed Rowles said.

Rowles admitted to having "two half schooners" of beer at 4pm but no more. That didn't jibe with other witnesses claiming he'd had a few whiskies as well before starting his run from Bulli into Wollongong.

A passenger on the Rowles bus testified that he had to tell Albert that his headlights were off, prompting him to fumble with the instrument panel while driving. That saw Albert stray onto the wrong side of the road and not pull up at stops to let passengers off.

Another passenger said Rowles' breath smelt of liquor and he was glassy-eyed.

Les Dion Sr was driving the Dion bus that night and testified that Rowles was on the wrong side of the road. So Les pulled off as far as he could, but Rowles still hit him.

Rowles admitted thinking the accident was a dream until he went back out of the house and saw the damage to the bus.

He denied in court he was weaving all over the road or smelt of liquor. He also claimed he had nothing to drink at Bulli at 6pm before starting his run into Wollongong. The magistrate found Rowles guilty of drink-driving and fined him £18 pounds, including costs.

"I regard this matter as serious," the magistrate said. "When a man drives a bus he is responsible for the lives of a number of people."

The serious nature of this case may have somehow led to an end of hostilities between the two families. From this point on, there appears to be no further newspaper reports of Dion vs Rowles court battles – which was probably a handy thing for their passengers.

Street betting

These days if you want to gamble on Keira Street, you have to go into one of the pubs and play the pokies or hang out in their "sports lounge". But once upon a time, you didn't even have to do that; it seemed like you could just find someone on the street to take your bet.

As long as you were near the Freemason's Hotel that once stood on the northwestern corner of the Keira-Crown intersection – where Wollongong Central is now. If you stood there in the 1920s and 1930s it seems you would have easily been able to place a bet; if the court appearances in that era are anything to go by. It wasn't unusual to see people hauled before a magistrate charged with street betting – and it always seemed to be the Freemason's Hotel where they stood.

One of them was Edwin Massey, who police claimed had been standing outside the pub in April 1929 giving people the odds on various horses. Then he walked into the pub, followed by the police who saw him reach under the public bar, take out a notebook and write in it.

The police officers left and went back to the station to ask the inspector what to do. He must have told them to go back, because that's where they were at 2pm, when they found two betting pads under the bar and a wad of betting slips in Massey's pockets.

Massey's lawyer tried to get the case thrown out on a technicality; as Massey was standing on the hotel steps when giving out the odds, he was in the hotel and not on the street and so could not be charged with street betting. The magistrate disagreed.

The lawyer's other defence strategy was to call several bar workers to the stand, along with another lunchtime drinker. They all testified that Massey stayed inside the hotel the whole time, so therefore he could not have been out on the street separating punters from their money. The magistrate disagreed with that too, finding Massey guilty and fining him a sizeable £20.

In 1933, Norman Clark was arrested for taking bets outside the hotel. Police said Clark took money from a man and then handed it onto another man, who made an entry in a book. For his part, Clark denied everything; he wasn't involved in SP betting and, hell, he wasn't even out in Keira Street that afternoon. He insisted he was sitting in the hotel having a quiet drink when a chap rushed in and threw a notebook and pencil at him.

It was only then that the coppers walked in and arrested him, Clark insisted. The magistrate didn't like what he heard and slapped Clark with a £20 fine too.

A year later Constable Lyons was in plainclothes and took up a position in the hall of the Freemasons. He later told the court he'd seen William Hicks on the street taking bets on a horse named Iconic. "I want you to come to the police station with me," Lyons told Hicks. The man asked why and was told he had been busted for street betting. "I'm stiff, I only started last Saturday and I'm pinched today," Hicks replied.

In his defence, Hicks said that, yes, he used to take bets but had given that up months ago. When the constable arrested him, he said, it came as quite a surprise. Perhaps not as much of a surprise as being found guilty and fined £5. Compared to the fines issued for other cases of street betting, it seems Hicks got off lightly.

The baby farmers

Sergeant Sheridan knew there was something wrong with John Makin. Born into a family of publicans, Makin decided to have a go at running one himself – though only after becoming a bankrupt in Sydney.

Back in his home town of Wollongong, in July 1872, he applied to become licensee of the Settlers Arms on the north-eastern corner of Keira and Crown streets. He was planning on changing the name to the Royal Alfred Hotel.

In the court hearing, Sgt Sheridan opposed Makin's grog licence, noting he worked on the wharf and therefore would not be likely to be on the premises. The sergeant also demanded Makin show his marriage certificate that stated he'd married Sarah Edwards the previous year. At the time, the police preferred their publicans to be married, under the belief they'd more responsible than single men. The magistrate agreed and Makin ended up coerced into bringing the piece of paper before the court – but he got his licence.

However, Sgt Sheridan kept his eye on Makin. Just four months later, he hauled the publican into court over a charge that he tried to break in a horse on a public street. However, the judge dismissed the case, deciding the sergeant had been mistaken in what he saw.

Not to worry, Sheridan got Makin back in court a month later, this time for allowing drunk and disorderly conduct at his establishment. Police had seen men fighting in the pub and Makin did almost nothing to stop them. A police witness told the court Makin came out onto the street and told him he wasn't going to try and break it up in case he got punched.

A drinker in the hotel told the court there were only two men fighting and Makin was too busy running the pub to break it up. Anyway, the fight only lasted a few minutes. Under cross-examination from Sgt Sheridan the witness lied through his teeth, suggesting the 15 people in the hotel at the time – including the two brawlers – were all stone-cold sober.

"It was well-known that his house was the last public house on the road out of the town," Makin's lawyer said, "and the result was that men got drunk elsewhere in town and while on their way home, called at defendant's house and very often made a disturbance, when the defendant was in no way responsible for the same."

Despite the lawyer's claim of drunk men on the premises clearly contradicted the hotel drinker's claim that no-one was drunk, the judge chose to dismiss the case. He had somehow decided there was no evidence Makin had seen the police officer outside the pub – even though the officer himself testified that they had a chat.

Sheridan had another go at Makin in October 1873, charging that he allowed gambling to take place at the Royal Alfred. Alexander McKenny said he had stayed at the hotel and, after the pub doors were closed, a game of two-up started in a room. McKenny insisted Makin was there and did nothing to stop it. McKenny said he lost £7 via the two-up and then another £6 when it fell from his pocket and others in the game picked it up and kept it.

A witness in the pub said he heard Makin tell the punters three or four times to get out. One of them tried to leave, the witness said, only to be pulled back by McKenny. Makin himself claimed he did everything he could to stop the gambling. Which didn't seem to be that much; there were two gamblers who weren't lodgers at the hotel and Makin was too scared to throw them out lest they punched him.

Yet again, the magistrate let Makin go free, finding him not guilty. But the Makins then decided to pack up and move to Sydney. Perhaps they were sick of being persecuted by Sgt Sheridan. Or perhaps Makin was doing a runner; in the short time he was publican at the Royal Alfred there were a number of court cases brought against him for owing money. It seems he might have been broke again.

In Sydney, Makin would become a man who horrified a city. In the early 1890s, the Makins turned to baby farming to make a living after John was injured in an accident. At the time there was an enormous stigma – both religious and social – with being a single mother. So some new mothers resorted to placing classified ads in newspapers asking for someone to look after their baby boy or girl, and offered to pay them.

Makin saw a chance to make some money, so the family started answering those ads to take in the babies – and the cash. But they weren't looking after the babies for long.

The Makins moved house regularly to avoid landlords demanding the rent. After the family had slunk away from their rented home in Burren Street, Macdonaldtown, the landlord had heard complaints about foul odours coming from the backyard. So he hired two men to dig in a new sewer pipe. They soon dug up a decomposing body, which they believed to be a cat. When a second one was unearthed soon afterward, the two men realised the bodies were those of babies.

An inquest was held and an open verdict was returned, meaning the Makins were not charged with anything. But the police weren't satisfied; days later they started digging in the Macdonaldtown backyard, finding another five bodies.

They arrested the Makins, while digging took place in the yards of other places the family had lived. Four more bodies were found at a George Street, Redfern, address and another in a vacant block at Zamia Street in the same suburb (police believe the Makins disinterred the body from their backyard and buried it in the empty lot).

After a trial, the Makins were found guilty of murder. While neither spoke at the trial, there was a police theory that the babies had been murdered with a hatpin through the heart. However the cause of death was never discovered – though poison seems a likely option.

Both were facing the death penalty but the Privy Council in Britain commuted Sarah's sentence to live in prison. No such mercy came John's way.

He made several appeals for clemency, and even his family got involved. In an odious fashion, they threw Sarah under a bus; she was the evil genius behind the scheme and John did whatever she asked.

"Your petitioners feel quite assured his wife was the originator of the crime for which he is under sentence," the *Mercury* reported of their claim for clemency from the Colonial Secretary, "whatever his connection with it may have been subsequently.

"That your petitioners firmly believe he would never have anything to do with such a crime had it not been for his wife." They added that Sarah was the "arch offender" and Makin "could be turned round his wife's finger". He made a lot of money, they said, but Sarah took it and drank it all (which didn't explain how Makin had become a bankrupt before he even met her).

The family's efforts got what they deserved – nothing. Makin was hanged in Darlinghurst jail on August 15, 1893. And Sgt Sheridan in Wollongong perhaps felt a sense of vindication that his feelings about Makin's character were finally proven to be correct.

The great fire

If the flames took hold, that row of shops on the edge of Keira Street could end up torching the city.

In the late 19th century, locals had been worried that those timber buildings along the southern side of Crown Street from the Keira Street corner down to Church Street were a disaster just waiting to happen. If a spark ignited the timbers in one building while a strong westerly was blowing, well, that could just turn the whole city to ashes.

That situation happened on August 25, 1895 – at least in part. It was a Sunday night, around 6.40pm. Angelina Osborne, wife of baker Alex, was in their home at the back of the Crown Street bakehouse when she saw flames coming from a room upstairs. She raised the alarm, but the fire was too busy feeding on the timbers – thanks to that strong westerly it soon spread to neighbouring businesses and sent flames shooting skyward that could be seen for some distance.

Those flames saw people run to the area, many

believing Royal Alfred Hotel on the northeastern Keira-Crown corner had caught alight. Secondary reports of the fire say it happened between Globe Lane and Church Street, but contemporary newspaper reports refer to Royal Alfred being across the road from the fire, which strongly suggests the fire travelled east from the Keira Street corner.

Fire crews tried to put out the blaze, as well as stop its spread, but to no avail. "The flames shot upward in terrific volume to a great height and for a considerable radius the darkness of night was dispelled by a brightness like that of day," the *Mercury* reported. "A fierce gust of wind which arose at this time swept a blinding cloud of sparks, cinders, smoke and dust right down the street, making it impossible for the firemen to face it."

While they fought the beast, some of the thousands who had been drawn to the flames helped the shop owners move furniture and stock out into the street in the hope of salvaging something from the destruction. Though the owners of Hobson and Co Chinese grocery objected to anyone removing any stock from the building. That probably wasn't a great idea, given the store stocked and sold kerosene, which gave the flames even more to feed on.

At one stage fears of a citywide conflagration rose up as the wind changed direction and a gust blew from the south, resulting in an arc of flame reaching out to devour the buildings on the other side of Crown Street. This time, the Royal Alfred really was on fire; flames were seen eating away an upper balcony. Firemen brandishing axes ran up the stairs to the balcony and began chopping away the burning sections while water was sprayed up from below. Just when their efforts looked to be futile against the fire, the winds died down permanently allowing the firemen to stop it from taking hold to the north. On the south side of the street, the fire stopped when it struck Gray's produce store, the only building in the block made of brick.

By 9pm, just over two hours after the alarm was raised, the fire was completely out. The toll it had taken in that time, however, was severe. As many as 11 buildings and shops were destroyed and one had to spare a thought for the unlucky Mr Pembroke, who had opened his confectionery shop just a day earlier. At least the bystanders had helped ferry out some of his stock before the flames could consume them.

There were also a few injuries on the night. Two men – by the name of Whitley and Webb - were upstairs in the Royal Alfred helping bring items to safety. For some reason, they found themselves out on the balcony and leant against the railing, somehow without noticing the other end was on fire. The railing couldn't take their weight and the pair tumbled three metres to the ground below. Whitley sprained his ankle while Webb opened a gash after landing head first. City physician Dr Lee stitched up Webb, who didn't seem to have any further injuries. A Mr Latiff managed to fall down a well while helping to fight the fire, bystanders jumping a fence to pull the unconscious man out. He had come close to drowning; after being taken to the Royal Alfred, he began vomiting up "filth and bad water", according to the *Mercury*. He too recovered from his injuries.

While there was no debating the fact the fire started at Osborne's bakery, no-one could say how it happened. It took hold in the upstairs room of Alexander McFarlane, a baker employed by Osborne, who was downstairs in the bakehouse at the time. "I do not know how the fire originated," he told the coroner's inquiry. "There was no sign of fire in the room when I left. I do smoke a pipe but had not been smoking that evening before I left the room."

The coroner handed down a finding that the fire had started at Osborne's bakery "but in what manner, whether accidental or otherwise, the evidence was not sufficient to show."

By the way, this wasn't the first time a fire had started at Osborne's place. The bakery nearly went up in flames three years earlier, in January 1892. Again, the baker on duty shrugged his shoulders and told the inquiry he had no idea how it started.

"I went to bed about 11 o'clock [the fire started at midnight]," baker Herbert Wall said. "Everything about the premises was alright then. I was in the bakehouse about 10.30 before the fire, the oven was not then alight and no fire to be seen anywhere about the premises. There was no person loitering about that I saw."

The finding was the same as in the 1895 fire; we know where it started but we don't know how. Though it did seem Osborne's employees needed to be more careful. One unexplained fire is alright, two is a tad concerning.

Going underground

For decades the only way someone could cross Keira Street was at ground level. Then, in 2013, work started to create a crossing in the sky and another underground. The crossings looked to link the existing Crown Central shopping centre with the soon-to-be completed Wollongong Central across the road – at the time both were owned by GPT.

The pedestrian bridge over Keira Street initially started out as one for cars, linking the car parks over the shopping centres. But somewhere along the line, saner heads prevailed and the car idea was nixed in favour of an enclosed pedestrian walkway.

To allow for the excavation of the tunnel, Keira Street between Crown and Market streets was restricted to two lanes – one in each direction. The digging included tearing up and then resurfacing the road, so the western lanes (and the footpath) were closed as the tunnellers dug halfway. Then, one night after the last buses had left the city, the jersey barriers were switched to close off the eastern lanes so digging underneath them could begin. A section of the footpath on the eastern side of Keira Street was also blocked off.

A few months after the eastern tunnelling began, plans were revealed to close that block of Keira Street. In both directions. For six months. The closure would allow for the construction of the streetside restaurant strip outside the GPT, with its wider foothpaths – and get it all over and done with faster. Then they could have the grand opening of the whole shebang, rather than opening the shops in late 2014 but with the restaurant strip unfinished. And the road would have to be closed again anyway because the footpath and associated works couldn't be done while cars drove by along Keira Street.

The full closure got the approval from Wollongong City Council, while businesses on the eastern side of the street were concerned. "I will still have a business," said Mylan restaurant's Nam Huynh, "but we've already lost a quarter of our business and I think we will lose more. I want it to be finished quickly."

Next-door at The Living Room, owner George Antoniou also wanted it to be done. "If it's going to help GPT finish the job quicker, I'm in favour of that," he said. "The quicker the better because the construction noise and other disruptions are getting too much."

The situation actually got slightly worse for those restaurants. Once the full closure took place pedestrians were redirected along the road surface of Keira Street, with the front doors of the restaurants difficult to find. Under the new system introduced mid-2014, Mr

Antoniou said the number of diners was sometimes so low he wondered whether it made more sense to close for the day.

"We've tried to embrace everything that's going on but it's hard when customer numbers are down due to noise and dust," he said. "The numbers have dropped quite significantly, and we knew there would be a drop – but that doesn't pay the bills at the end of the day."

Keira Street was also a thoroughfare for the city's buses travelling to and from the northern suburbs. With the street between Smith and Crown fenced off, buses had to be re-routed down Smith and Kembla streets and the associated bus stops relocated. Though Les Dion from Dion's Bus Service said no access to Keira Street was actually better than the two lanes their bus drivers had been dealing with in the early stages of the tunnel construction.

"We can run more to our timetable because they're not being held up at the Keira-Crown streets intersection," Mr Dion said. "The timetable will remain the same and we'll actually have a better chance of complying with it, given that we'll be getting around that bottleneck."

The planned October 1, 2014, reopening of Keira Street was missed; partially because of heavy rains delayed works. And also because it seemed safer to keep the road closed for the grand opening, given there would be people everywhere.

"There's going to be a lot of pedestrian traffic in and around the centre," GPT development manager Steve

Turner said, "and it's not like the existing centre [Crown Central] where there's a mall in between."

The section of Keira Street reopened on Monday, October 13 – the same day as the traffic lights at Keira and Victoria streets were switched on. Mr Dion was pleased with the improvements, which included the new western bus bay and the city's first bus lane on the eastern side, which would relieve the "choke point" of Keira Street.

"It just gives us a little bit of extra wiggle room to pass through Keira Street more effectively," he said. "We not picking up passengers in the transit mall any more, we're picking them up in front of GPT. That makes for a much more efficient journey, so far as on-time running goes.

"It is very significant because what used to happen is we would pick up passengers in the transit mall and then try and get out of there, getting caught behind other buses and stuck in traffic."

And The Living Room's Mr Antoniou was happy the road was reopened and the drilling across the road had ceased. It meant an end to cleaning up the concrete dust customers tracked in off the street. "Now I don't have to buy a new mop every month," he said. "It's one less chore."

Drive-by on Keira Street

"There were two distinct bangs," the witness said. "I thought it was just a car backfiring then I turned around and saw this fellow drop to the ground. Another guy screamed and grabbed his stomach and all this blood started pouring out."

It was just after 3.30pm on February 23, 1999, outside the Monsoon restaurant on Keira Street. One man had walked up to another, loaded a shotgun he'd been carrying for weeks and fired twice. One shot went down Keira Street. The second hit his target Vedran Ravnjak in the stomach. A witness saw him sitting in the gutter, with his hands trying to literally hold himself together. The gunman then raced across Keira Street and escaped in a white four-wheel drive.

Ravnjak was rushed to hospital, a bedsheet wrapped around his abdomen. Inside his body the gunshot pellets had spread to the liver, gall bladder and small and large intestines. It was what the doctors called an "unsurvivable wound" and Ravnjak died in hospital.

The gunman's first shot did some damage as well. Businessman Martin Anstee had just stepped out of Monsoon – his friend was still inside squaring up the bill – when he was hit in the back with 35 pellets. A nine-year-old schoolboy and seven other bystanders were also hit. In a stroke of good fortune, a first aid course was under way right across the road; after instructor Ian Gray looked out the window at the carnage, he grabbed his first-aid kit and rushed across the road. All of the bystanders survived, many of them had the pellets left in their body because surgery carried with it the risk of nerve damage.

The city had never seen such a brazen shooting in one of its main streets. In searching for an explanation, some feared it marked the start of some sort of drug war. At the time of his shooting Ravnjak had been out on bail over drug offences after police allegedly found amphetamines and marijuana inside a stolen car he was driving. An underworld source told the *Mercury* fights used to be settled with fists but now firearms were being used.

He claimed the word on the street was that Ravnjak – known to many as Veg – had been executed by another drug dealer. "Most people who knew Veg from the drug scene aren't surprised by the fact he was murdered, they just can't believe where it happened," the source said.

"Killing him like that, with so many witnesses around, doesn't seem too smart. The guys who did this were just asking to get caught."

But the killing wasn't related to drugs. The truth came

out when Zlatan Popovic was arrested in Sydney just five days after the shooting. It had been sparked by a love triangle. The long-time friends fell out when Ravnjak suspected his girlfriend and Popovic were romantically involved. From there, Popovic alleged Ravnjak made repeated threats to his family, including a promise to tie Popovic up and kill his mother in front of him and then torture his son. The killer alleged Ravnjak would call up to 50 times a day in the weeks before the killing, making threats and asking if his girlfriend was there.

In a March bail hearing, police alleged Popovic dug up a sawn-off shotgun that had been buried at Mt Keira and began carrying it around with him. "I do not go anywhere without the shotgun," police alleged Popovic told them. "I had it loaded on a number of occasions and if I saw him I was going to shoot him."

On Keira Street in the week after the shooting, Monsoon itself was very quiet. Normally the popular newly-opened restaurant was packed for lunch but there were plenty of empty tables. Some other owners along that strip, however, reported a boost in business as customers came in asking about the shooting.

The Illawarra Business Chamber decided to stage a symbolic reclaiming of Keira Street. "We can't rely on the powers that be to do it because we know our local area better than anyone," chamber president Phil McGavin said. "We can't allow things to keep going the way they have been – businesses just can't keep replacing their windows every second week. Wollongong is not the Dodge City of the south – it's a great place to live."

The reclaiming took place on Tuesday, March 2, with around 200 people marching along Keira Street from the mall to Smith Street and back. "Today we start what I believe will be a very strong push in returning the city to the standards we all enjoyed in the past," chamber member David Morgan Williams said.

Popovic's trial began in June 2000, with the shooter's barrister Peter Zahra mounting the defence that the repeated threats from Ravnjak had taken their toll. "At the time of the killing the accused was in an extreme state of fear," Zahra told the court.

In response the Crown Prosecutor Paul Conlon said this had nothing to do with self-defence, saying Popovic planned to "wipe out" Ravnjak if the chance presented itself. "He made sure of that by always having the weapon at hand," Conlon said. "The deceased did not present any real physical threat to the accused. He merely became an extreme nuisance."

During the trial, the police played footage of the interview with Popovic shortly after he was arrested. In it he said he felt no regret for shooting Ravnjak. "He has burned me so much that it does not bother me what happened to him. I have no remorse for that now."

Though there was remorse for the bystanders who still had his shotgun pellets inside them. "I didn't think that the gun was going to do that much damage," he told police. "All my remorse is for the people I found out later that I got while firing the shots at Veg."

Popovic said he and Ravnjak had spotted each other on Keira Street that fateful day, "and I knew he would probably want to get me as much as I wanted to get him".

He called out to Ravnjak, asking if he intended on carrying out those threats he'd made on the phone. Ravnjak assured Popovic that he would.

"I got the gun out of the bag," Popovic said. "He watched me load it. Then when he noticed what it was he sort of came towards me with his right hand." Popovic swung the gun, hitting Ravnjak and discharging the first shot. "Then I shot him straight in the stomach."

The woman who made up the third side of the love triangle testified that Popovic had put Ravnjak in hospital after the latter turned up at a house where she and Popovic were five weeks before the shooting.

The two men had gone outside and began fighting. At one stage, Ravnjak was on the ground unconscious and Popovic was kicking him, she said. In his own testimony, Popovic said Ravnjak had pulled a knife on him at the start of the fight.

Ravnjak spent six days in hospital and Popovic claimed the harassing phone calls continued as soon as he was discharged. "He said 'listen to me you arsehole. I guarantee you that I will kill you. Putting me in hospital is nothing. I will come back harder. I am going to follow you around. Be wary. Wherever you go I will be there. I have friends watching'."

Popovic also told the court, the Keira Street incident wasn't the first time he had fired shots at Ravnjak. Three days earlier he claimed Ravnjak had called him and at his mother's house and told him to come outside. When he stepped out he saw Ravnjak and what he was sure was a pistol in his hand. Popovic was also carrying, and let loose with five shots from his .357 Magnum as Ravnjak pedalled away.

When he saw Ravnjak on the street that day, Popovic said he was "in fear". "I was scared because I didn't know what was going to happen," he said. "I thought he would come over, probably for a go at me. Shoot me, stab me, kill me. That was in my mind."

What else was in his mind? "My head told me that I had to shoot him."

The jury went behind closed doors for three and a half days. They were able to reach a guilty decision on the nine counts of malicious wounding; they related to the bystanders, and Popovic had admitted to them during the trial. However, they were split 11-1 on the charge or murder – to which Popovic had pleaded not guilty.

A second trial began in March 2001, just over a year after the shooting, with Popovic again pleading not guilty. That trial was aborted later that month after a death in the family of Popovic's barrister.

Soon after that, the Crown accepted Popovic's guilty plea for manslaughter, recognising that his defence of provocation had been strengthened by the weight of evidence heard in the previous trial.

In December, he would be sentenced to 10 years' jail. The sentence was backdated to the day of his arrest in February 1999. The three-year sentence on the malicious wounding charges would be served concurrently.

In his decision Justice Barry O'Keefe accepted the cumulative effects of the threats and harassment had led

Popovic to lose self-control. However, he dismissed the defence claims that there was no degree of premeditation.

"With all the circumstances surrounding the shooting, I am of the belief that the prisoner had intended to kill Mr Ravnjak when they confronted each other in Keira Street," Justice O'Keefe said.

Monsoon restaurant, which became associated with the shooting in people's minds, kept going for another eight years. In 2001, rival Vietnamese restaurant Mylan opened up across the road, next-door to what was the city's first sushi train restaurant (roughly where the Guzman franchise now sits). In 2008 they bought out Monsoon and moved across the road and have been there ever since.

Michael Bolt

When the name Michael Bolt is mentioned, most people in town think of the Illawarra Steelers. Which is understandable as he has a strong connection to the team. As captain of the third grade side in 1982, he was the first Steelers player to take the field when he led that side onto Wollongong Showground for its debut match. He holds the record for the most top grade matches for the Steelers at 182 and, when he retired in 1990 he had played 187 consecutive games across all grades for the Steelers, a league record at the time.

But he has a longer connection to Keira Street, which goes as far back as when he was just 15 years old and working as a dishpig at the Loong Chee restaurant, which would later be the home of hatted dining establishment Caveau.

In 1985 he switched from being a washer-upper to an owner, establishing popular nightspot Cousins in Keira Street with cousins Kevin Cooney and Andrew Farrar – he remembered working there late and having to head to

Keira Street

Steelers training for 7am.

"There were a lot of places where you just went and got drunk late and that was all," he told the *Mercury*. "We wanted to have a place where people could enjoy a bit more live music and we would often have two or three live bands.

"It worked extremely well and within a couple of weeks [of opening] we were packed every night and some New Year's Eves we had queues 250 metres long just to get in there."

He remembered the strip of Keira Street from Market to Smith was very different in those days. For instance, the Illawarra Hotel was a long way from the bright, open space it is today.

"Also, Amigos had been there for years and was an institution," he said. "There were also a few Chinese restaurants but the best thing was Mamma's [at 108 Keira Street].

"It had the best schnitzels – they were huge and everyone remembers them. We used to finish up at the club and then go to Mamma's until about six o'clock in the morning."

A few years later he moved down to lower Crown Street, where the Glasshouse was and set up Pigdogs Café. This was years before hip cafes like Lee and Me and Lower East lobbed up.

"It was perfect," Bolt said, "but it was too far ahead of Wollongong. It was a groovy café for 1991 with concrete floors, washed walls and an industrial feeling with no ceilings."

But he soon went back to Keira Street, to set up Metro on the corner of Victoria Street. "Metro was similar to Lorenzo's, it was that small and intimate sort of bar and restaurant where everyone knew each other," he said. "My ex-wife was doing all the cooking and she was a fantastic chef."

However, it again seemed to be a bit ahead of the curve. It stood out on Keira Street without similar restaurants surrounding it. This was an era before that block of Keira became known as Eat Street.

Then he went to North Beach and set up Stingrays, realising it was too much running two places at the same time. The next step was to leave those spots and set up his best-known venture, the Five Islands Brewery on the eastern side of the entertainment centre.

Again, it was ahead of its time, brewing and selling his own beer in 2001, years before the craft beer boom hit Australian shores. There is a school of thought that Five Islands brewed and sold the first IPA in Australia, which if true, is no mean feat.

Five Islands went into receivership in 2010, eventually being replaced by the Illawarra Brewing Company. In 2012 Bolt headed back to his old stomping ground of Keira Street to set up Red Square a few doors down from the Smith Street corner. After he came up with the name, he chose to build a drinks menu around it; with a Russian-sounding name, vodka made perfect sense.

At the time of opening, the small bar scene was starting to take off on the city as people realised they enjoyed another option than just going to the pub. "Little

Prince and Yours and Owls are a couple of examples of this style of venue," he said, "which has been popular in Melbourne and other cities for many years and now Wollongong residents are enjoying it too."

In 2018, he looked across the road at a spot next door to Debutante (which also used to house Lorenzo's) that was a bank at one stage – the vault is still there.

With former partner Alli Dawson and daughter Zoe Bolt, they set up a gin bar called Juniper. They picked the site after Lorenzo Pagnan had asked if he knew anyone who might be interested in the hole-in-the-wall site.

With the gin craze just kicking off, Bolt felt the time was right. "I had been wanting to do a gin bar for a while and that's how it started. We have 50 gins to start with and we are planning to grow that to 100."

Stalling a shopping centre

In 1975, the city welcomed the Crown Central shopping centre, on the northeastern corner of Keira and Crown streets. But the two-level centre was a long time coming, and almost didn't make it – thanks to a single shop owner holding out for a better payday.

By 1971, Abbey Orchard Property Investments had acquired all the properties it needed to build the centre – except one. And that one holdout stalled the project for more than a year.

Peggy Hunt had a small fashion store on Crown Street, right where Crown Central was going to be built. The developer had nabbed all the other properties, some which were standing there empty, but Peggy kept trading. And kept holding the developer at bay.

The sticking point was unhappiness with the price Abbey Orchard was offering. They'd first offered $42,500 and then took it up to $125,000 but she wanted $500,000. Without that half-million, the fashion store was going to stay put.

It was really unsettling the city council, where a

committee in June 1971 resolved that if the selling price couldn't be resolved, it would compulsorily acquire Peggy's shop.

"When the owner is prepared to sell, at terms which are somewhat extortionate, the council has a responsibility to come in on the matter," Lord Mayor Ford said. "I would hate to see this $15 million development lost because of one small stumbling block."

It took more than a year to overcome the impasse. On September 29, 1972, the *Mercury* reported that the developer had finalised a deal with Peggy Hunt – though the final price wasn't mentioned.

With plans for Crown Central already approved, the developer mentioned they might even rent out some of those vacant shops in the lead-up to Christmas. "All the problems are now over and Crown Street will be getting a new lease of life," new Lord Mayor Parker crowed.

But he crowed too soon. For that small fashion store wasn't the final hurdle – not even because it had a tenancy deal that allowed it to stay put until June 1973. That hurdle would be the fault of the developer. On April 4, 1973, Abbey Orchard said it had decided to review its plan, which the city council feared meant Crown Central was dead and buried.

"We have been told by the company that it will be September before anything can be made public about its new plans," Lord Mayor Parker said. "The company said it is reviewing its plans and conducting a feasibility study."

The main reason to fear the cancellation of the project was that, like Wollongong Central years later, the council and the business community had pinned their hopes on a new shopping centre giving the city a big economic boost.

The developer didn't make the city wait until September; it unveiled its new plans later in April 1973. The project had been slashed in half – from $15 million down to $7 million. That massive cost saving came as a result of scrapping the plan to build a central tower over the two-storey shopping complex that would be used as a motel.

"It is believed all other essential features of the original plan have been retained," the *Mercury* reported. "A department store, two shopping plaza levels, a mezzanine floor, specialty shops and two floors of car parking."

Rather than be grateful a $7 million development was happening in the city, business people complained about the missing $8 million. And it would take forever to build, they whinged.

Well, they got that wrong. Shoppers were walking around the new centre in 1975 – and it would still be in use 50 years later.

Keira Street

The Illawarra Hotel

If the people of Thirroul in the 1930s weren't such wowsers, the Illawarra Hotel might never have gotten a liquor licence. The licence the city hotel operates under was originally transferred from the Lake Illawarra Hotel in Brownsville in 1937, though not before licensee Alfred Ball (or Bell, newspapers of the time gave him conflicting surnames) tried his luck at Thirroul.

In 1936, the city's licencing bench heard his application to transfer the Brownsville licence to a new hotel in Main Street, Thirroul (which is now likely known as Lawrence Hargrave Drive). The Thirroul locals had lodged a stack of objections; the new pub would disturb the peace of the community, it was too close to churches, too close to shunting yards, it was not needed in Thirroul and not in the suburb's best interests. Oh, and Brownsville needed the licence anyway so it should stay there.

While the shunting yard excuse may seem to us to be a nitpicking excuse, at the time pubs also offered accommodation; that objection was based on the noise generated by the trains and the effect it would have on guests in the hotel. The shunting yard claim didn't wash with the bench, but the decline in takings for Ryans Hotel – already established in Thirroul – did. The bench found that, if that hotel wasn't raking in the cash, it suggested there wasn't the local appetite for a second pub.

A year later Ball (or Bell) was back, this time looking to transfer the licence to an as-yet unbuilt hotel on the corner of Keira and Market streets. Unlike today, where councils and other bodies have qualms about the size of developments, in 1937, they actually felt the Illawarra Hotel wasn't big enough; the two-storey 24-room hotel needed another floor such was the demand for accommodation in the city.

It was so well-known that even the police testified to that effect. "Sergeant Lee said during July, when he was on night duty about 50-55 motorists had approached him regarding hotel accommodation," the *South Coast Times* reported. "There was a need for at least 150 additional bedrooms in the town, not necessarily all in the one hotel but spread out over the whole number."

The lawyer representing Tooth and Co, the owner of the proposed Illawarra Hotel, said his clients could go up another level and add another 20 rooms. But if they were going to have to do that to get this transfer of licence over the line, then other hotels in the city should be told to increase their accommodation as well. Whether that was in the bench's power is unclear, though they did approve the licence transfer – and it survived an appeal by the

Keira Street

Brownville locals who felt they needed the liquor licence to stay in the suburb.

So on November 17, 1938, the Hotel Illawarra (as it was known at the time) poured its first beers. And the *Mercury* couldn't help itself, going rather overboard in describing every little detail of the place.

"The building embodies the latest ideas in modern architectural construction and is carried out in cream brick while the interior decorations reflect the same key note of simplicity, the walls being in cream throughout," the *Mercury* reported.

Furnishings and carpeting were supplied by Anthony Horderns, "which supply the tasteful harmony of colour and design characteristic of modern decorative idiom" – whatever that means. The ground floor carpet was an Axminister "in a small Persian design patterned rust and blue on a sharp fawn background". Upstairs the carpet was blue and rust coloured, except for the bedrooms which were in rose, burgundy, blue, green and rust shades.

"The furnishings harmonise and curtains have been provided in Italian damask in rust and beige," the *Mercury* gushed. "The lounge is curtained in green velours well suited to the hotel situation which is on the main road to Wollongong and surrounded by a magnificent panorama of hills and green countryside."

The publican was Hilda Condon, who led a team that included her sister, two daughters and a female-dominated staff. No doubt the female presence helped keep some of the male drinkers in line, lest they offended the fairer sex. It probably also helped that Condon willingly held bottles of beer behind the counter for regulars to pick up when the clock struck six – early closing was still in force. The bottles were discreetly wrapped and Condon even trained her staff to refer to it as wine to skirt the licencing laws.

Condon was known to skirt other rules as well. Publicans were required to put methyl violet in their drip trays. The substance would change the colour of the spilled beer; the intent was to stop pubs from pouring the dregs from the tray back into glasses or jugs. In 1941, Condon was busted by a Health Department inspector, who found trays at the Illawarra with no colouring.

Condon wasn't on her own in this; the inspector had also caught out the Royal Hotel in town, Port Kembla's Commercial and Steelworks hotels in what seemed to a sweep of Wollongong pubs.

While the female publican and staff may have smoothed out some of the rougher edges of their clientele, it's no surprise that some men couldn't behave themselves once they were a few beers deep. Punters from the Hotel Illawarra regularly appeared in the city's court.

As was the case with drinkers at other pubs, some were done for indecent language. Though there were some more interesting incidents.

John Rowles was on the punt at the hotel in 1939 and some other drinkers noticed he'd won some money. So they followed him out and told him to "shell out and shell out quick or you're on the knuckle".

Just a few months later George Gray and Charles McGuire were charged with beating up Thomas Dale at the back of the hotel. He'd gone for a short walk and had just returned to the hotel when he was attacked – "I was pretty drunk" he admitted in court.

Later at the police station, McGuire was shown to Dale, who insisted he wasn't the man who whacked him. Perhaps assuming Dale was too drunk at the time to make an accurate identification, the court found McGuire guilty and sentenced him to jail. How Gray fared went unreported.

The year 1949 saw Henry Bastock labelled a "king-hit expert" after flooring Lloyd Tyler at the pub, even though the victim had just bought him a few beers.

One of the more unusual instances took place upstairs in 1949. Thomas Horsfall had been found in the hallway and falsely claimed to be a guest. Staff member Mabel O'Meara raised the alarm when she spied a pair of her pink panties on the floor at his feet.

Turned out Horsfall had more items of women's undergarments on him, as well as jewellery pilfered from Margaret Condon's rooms. He ended up being sentenced to a three-year good behaviour bond and was told by the magistrate to steer clear of the booze.

By the late 1980s, the Hotel Illawarra had seen better days. The back bar, where I spent quite a few nights while studying at uni, was dark and one wag described it as place where the toilets smelled better than the bar. The aroma and the lighting were better out on the Keira-Market streets corner, where the front bar was home to a number of pool tables. With glass doors and windows all the way around, you could see the passing parade outside while waiting for your 20-cent piece to make its way through the queue for a game.

The hotel got a minor makeover in the early 2000s but it wasn't until new owners Ryan and Nikki Atchison took over that the place got a massive overhaul. In January 2020, the Illawarra (the "hotel" was dropped) closed its doors so that an effective gutting of the interior could take place. The plan was to open the doors in March 2020 but COVID put an end to all that. Premier Gladys Berejiklian shut down all the pubs (and quite a few other things as well), which meant the new Illawarra Hotel had to wait.

Though Ryan Aitchison said it wasn't a bad thing that the lockdown came before they'd even opened up. "If we had have launched the month before and had to shut down then that would have been catastrophic," he said.

They did get to open for a while, albeit with reduced capacity due to social distancing but the second lockdown in June buggered things up again. By August, when the lockdown was extended, the Illawarra Hotel (the "hotel" bit was back) had to get rid of the beer they had on tap. So they sold it at $10 a litre, which saw people queuing up along Keira Street with a range of receptacles. The smart ones brought growlers from breweries while other made do with eskies, empty two-litre milk bottles and kitchen pots.

"We didn't think lockdown was going to go so long." Nikki said. "We've been keeping an eye on our stock and as the weeks of lockdown go by, most of our stock only has three or four weeks of use-by date left so we decided to have this event. If we'd held onto the stock we were looking at losing $10-$15,000, which we can't afford to do right now."

On October 11, with the vaccination rate at 70 per cent, the chance for discount beer was gone. But punters would be able to order a beer over the bar, with what had been tagged "Freedom Day" seeing those wise double-vaxxed people able to go into pubs.

Ryan Aitchison said the second lockdown hurt more than the first because they were gearing up for a big end to the year. But now they'd have to build that momentum all over again - and do it on reduced turnover thanks to the 4sqm rule.

"We can kind of tread water [when we were closed] because of the government support," he said. "We're more worried about opening when all our costs come back, which is a lot. When we re-open our trade is only going to be around 25 per cent. Once that [government support] stops and we need to open our doors and pay our staff and creditors and whatnot – that's the part we're not looking forward to."

They managed to get through that, enough to look to carry out even more renovations. In May 2024, the Atchisons lodged plans to redevelop the long derelict accommodation upstairs, building a kitchen, bistro and lounge on the first floor and a private dining room on the next level up.

Incidentally, there was one big name change that went

further than reversing the order of "Illawarra" and "Hotel", or dropping the "hotel" altogether. In March 2022, it became the Volkanovski Hotel, in honour of local MMA champion Alexander Volkanovski. They even scrapped off the lettering outside and paid someone to replace it with "The Volkanovski Hotel". As a PR exercise, it worked wonders; giving the pub at the corner of Keira and Market streets worldwide exposure on TV and online. The six-week promotion effectively ended when The Volk beat Chan Sung Jung in his title defence – and of course plenty of people turned up at The Volkanovski Hotel to watch the fight.

Keira Street

A lost piece of art

For a short while, if you stood at the Keira-Burelli street traffic lights waiting for the walk signal to head south, you could pass the time by gazing at the city's first public mural.

What is now the Crown Gateway car park was once known as the PDS Building. It should be mentioned there are actually two different car parks here. The first – the one with the Kenny Street entrance - was opened back in 1972. It was the first multi-storey car park in the city and was deemed such a strange new thing that WIN TV chose run a story explaining how it worked. In the mid-1980s, a second carpark was built right next-door, for the Gateway shopping centre. The fact they are two separate parking lots, built more than a decade apart tends to surprise people, but explains why it's not possible for a car to drive from one side to the other. But we'll get back to the car park in a page or so.

In May 1982, the Public Art Squad's Rodney Monk got to work on the mural that would cover the 300-square metre northern wall of the PDS building and due to be finished in a few months. "Mr Monk said anyone could contribute in Wollongong's first public 'paint splashing'," the *Mercury* reported, "provided the theme was followed."

That theme was initially explained as depicting "aspects of the city's way of life". But the finished product seemed to focus on the then Lord Mayor Frank Arkell – back before people knew his dark secrets.

Smack in the middle of the work was an artist's impression of Arkell, arms folded and wearing a dark suit and what appears to be a pink shirt underneath. Located in the centre of the work, with industrial girders rising away on either side, the eye is drawn to the Lord Mayor. It's almost like he'd commissioned a self-portrait. It must have been unpleasant for his victims to see that image of Arkell every time they came into town.

Inside the building was a new artistic endeavour called Theatre South, which started staging shows there a month or so after the mural work started. "Wollongong has needed a permanent drama venue for quite some time," Theatre South's Des Davies said.

But the life of the first public mural – and the first home of Theatre South – would be short. In May 1985, the wrecking ball was put to work and the PDS building and mural were no more. The Kern Corporation, developer of the Gateway shopping centre, had always said using the PDS site for a car park was a non-negotiable part of building the centre. No car park, no Gateway.

The mural was dead and buried, but Theatre South

survived. After some justified panic about what to do, the theatre company ended up developing a new home at Coniston, near the train station, which it occupied for decades afterwards.

Glen Humphries

Going to the movies

The Wollongong CBD has a lot of things to offer; but a movie theatre isn't one of them. You want to go see a film rather than stream something to your phone? Well, head to Warrawong or Shellharbour – that's the best we can do.

It never used to be like that – the CBD was oversupplied by movie houses. There was the Civic Theatre – now the town hall – the Globe, the Savoy and not one but two cinemas in Keira Street. The first was the Crown Cinema, which was located roughly at the northern end of where Wollongong Central hangs over Keira Street.

It opened in 1911 as an open-air theatre – which was far more common than you'd expect. Though it meant theatregoers' noses may have been assailed by the stockyards next-door. And it was big; 1500 seats. The place must have been selling out because a year later, they added another 500 seats and decided to put a roof over the whole thing.

Keira Street

An architectural firm was tasked in 1920 to design a new theatre, which of course meant they had to increase the number of seats, which went up to 2044 when the doors opened again in 1921.

More alterations came in 1926, and the seating climbed again to 2456. A decade later another renovation, though this time they brought the seating down, to 2354. The high number of seats makes sense when you realise there was no TV back then. If you wanted to see pictures move, then you had to go to the movies.

When it closed in 1965 after screening John Wayne's *Circus World* ("dismally trite", said the *New York Times*), there was some mild outrage with the *South Coast Times* bemoaning the fact it left the CBD with only one cinema. Think yourself lucky – one is better than none. All furnishings and fixtures were sold at auction and the Crown Theatre remained empty until the early 1970s, when Coles demolished it to build a new store.

The other Keira Street theatre is still there – the Regent, though it's been quite a few years since it showed a movie. But the place still occupies a special place in people's hearts; in part because the interior still resembles the glory days of cinema theatres in the first half of the 20th century. That saw marble flooring, loads of seats, and a feeling of glamour. Though the Regent must have been seen as something special back when it was under construction in the 1950s; back then people mistook that huge, beautiful foyer as the cinema – there was a shock when they realised the actual screen and seating would be *behind* that.

The theatre was the brainchild of Herbert Jones, who bought the parcel of land it sits on back in 1934. However it took quite a while to get the theatre off the ground, in part due to issues around raising the funds. An early prospectus to drum up some cash showed the initial plans included an open courtyard in front of the theatre. That would eventually be roofed and become that glorious entry foyer.

Jones never got to see the project start; he passed away in 1943, seven years before his family got construction under way. And then it was another seven years before the theatre opened for business in 1957. In those years it became a home for the arthouse style of film – the travelling film festivals called the place home for a long time. It was also the place to go for special midnight screenings of new release films; a number of the second series of *Star Wars* films had midnight openings on the first day of release, with theatregoers dressed up as their favourite characters.

In the early 2000s, when the theatre's future came under threat from developers, the city fought back. In 2002 Lend Lease had eyes on redeveloping the section of the city bordered by Keira, Church, Market and Burelli streets, at the behest of the then owner of Wollongong Central and the Gateway.

Part of the early stage plans was for a 10-screen cinema complex. What that meant for the Regent was up in the air. Lendlease's Robert Lewis didn't exactly instil confidence in the community. "Whether we keep the façade or incorporate a theatre into our overall plans will be decided by what the community wants," he said.

The National Trust waded in, with deputy director of conservation Graham Quint recognising the Regent's importance and looking to include it on the trust's register. "The Regent Theatre is an extremely important part of Wollongong's heritage and represents a living history," he said.

Local film-maker and director of the city's Short Sited Film Festival David Kemmery was similarly unimpressed with the possibility the Regent could go. "While I support the concept of revitalising the CBD, I cannot understand why the Regent Cinema cannot be an integral part of the process," Kemmery said. "It is a unique theatre that provides a venue for films that are a little different and not mainstream."

With the threat of redevelopment still hanging over the Regent two years later, the January 2004 passing of theatre owner, Jones' daughter Rona Milgrove, further fuelled fears for the Regent's future. The South Coast Labour Council applied to the state government to place an interim heritage order to block any development, though the request was knocked back due to there being no immediate threat to the theatre. The city council also called on Lendlease to show its cards; the group responded with "we don't have any firm plans".

The unions took matters into their own hands, placing a green ban on any demolition. CFMEU assistant state secretary Peter Zaboyak said the theatre "was a unique part of Wollongong's history and heritage".

"This ban will stop any sudden moves to demolish the

place and should be a clear message to any midnight buyers that come along that the community will have a say in any future development," he said.

The immediate future of the Regent was for it to be sold. It went on the market in October 2004, prompting the state government to place it on the NSW Heritage Register before any new owner took over. That new owner turned out to be the Gateway City Church, which was in need of a new home.

"We've just outgrown the facility," senior minister Scott Hanzy said of the church's Victoria Street home. "We've been growing by 10 to 20 members per month. Building something was our first priority but there was nothing available in the city."

The congregation weren't the only people who got to use the place, either. An expensive refurbishment turned the theatre into a live music venue by 2007, leading to the likes of Missy Higgins, Paul Kelly and Hoodoo Gurus performing there.

Evan Davis from band bookers Harbour Agency said the venue brought something special to the city. "It really helps generate a flexibility and diversity in Wollongong," Davis said. "It gives artists and agents more options – you can have that intimate theatre experience instead of automatically going to WIN Entertainment Centre. It's a definite advantage for Wollongong to have a venue that offers that."

In 2017, the Gateway City Church had gotten even bigger, managing to outgrow the 1200-seat theatre. They had put it on the market previously, in 2009, but that came to nothing as the church changed its mind. "We had outgrown the building in some respects," Hanzy said of the 2009 attempted sale, "and we just felt we needed to look at the next step. But we loved the position, and it's a great building. So we kept it on for a little while and then we ended up saying 'we want to stay here'. This time we've definitely outgrown it."

In mid-2018 Sydney live entertainment group Century Venues took an option to buy the Regent. Executive director Greg Khoury said they were testing the waters to see if there was enough interest in reopening it as a music venue. "We see the opportunity to bring to Wollongong many of the national and international acts and performers we present in Sydney," Khoury said.

But that option expired in May 2019, with Century unable to proceed with plans to purchase, though Khoury still saw value in the Regent. "To create a theatre with such an ambiance and architectural merit in such a premium location would today be impossible," he said.

A Wollongong and Sydney based consortium – later revealed to include Yours & Owls – picked up the venue in 2020 with a view to turning it into the city's version of the Enmore Theatre. In a development application to make changes including the removal of seating and adding a few bars, the future plans for the Regent were clear.

"This will provide the ability to host live music, plays, dances, lectures, stand-up comedy and film," the application said, "equipping the venue for a more contemporary form of live entertainment and bringing life back to the Regent Theatre. A similar precedent to this proposal can be found at the Enmore Theatre."

Work was slow, with further internal changes – albeit minor – flagged in 2024. When it finally throws open the doors again, the city will find out if it was worth the wait.

Keira Street

Fine dining

Keira Street has been home to not one, but two restaurants that were hatted for a long, long time. "Hatted" refers to the *Good Food Guide* anointing your place as something quite special.

First in line was Lorenzo Pagnan's Due Mezzi, which he moved from Bulli into town in 1999. The restaurant held onto its hat until 2006, when a change in name (to Lorenzo's Diner) and concept didn't impress the judges. Though Pagnan didn't care too much; "We are doing good business, but obviously it isn't fine dining like it used to be," he said. "We wanted to demystify dining."

He stayed in Keira Street – changing the name again to The Cheeky Fig – until 2019 when his former chef Daniel Sherley took over the lease and opened Debutante.

That last year Pagnan had a hat for his place, a new restaurant across the road picked one up – and held onto it for 15 years. In 2004, Peter and Nicola Sheppard opened up Caveau. Peter had started a mechanical engineering degree at uni but packed it in to chase his dream of becoming a chef. He served an apprenticeship at Sydney's Banc Restaurant before opening up his own place in Huskisson and later moving to Keira Street.

Caveau was tagged as "modern French", though that did bring with it the inevitable questions about frogs' legs. "We describe it as modern French because when you say French, people think about snails and frogs' legs and it's not that at all," Nicola said. "There's never any snails or frogs' legs on the menu; it's taking traditional methods and traditional techniques but actually serving it in a modern way."

Caveau landed its first hat in 2005, just a year after opening. "We aim for the quality people used to go to Sydney for," Peter said, "so this is a great compliment and means we're doing the right thing." When yet another hat came in 2007, the judge's comments seemed like a backhander at Wollongong – and forgot all about Pagnan's nine consecutive hats across the road. "It feels like a minor miracle to find food this good and service so unobtrusively stylish on the gritty main drag of the Gong," the judges said, unconsciously showing their own snobbish preconceptions of the city.

Though by 2009, it seemed as though locals still hadn't cottoned onto the five-time hatted restaurant in Keira Street. "Our customers are dining first class for economy prices," Nicola said. "The press gets it, the critics get it but the people of Wollongong just aren't showing up." A few years later, they were still having to challenge the idea that people could eat well without leaving town.

Keira Street

"Wollongong's mindset is that if you want something special you have to go to Sydney," Peter said. "It's true we don't have the Opera House or the Bridge so we have to work quite hard at what we want to achieve here."

The Sheppards decided to branch out in 2015, opening up a second restaurant just down the road in a large space opposite the Illawarra hotel. Called MoChi, it was a Cantonese-inspired dumpling house, serving the food they liked. "When we opened Caveau, we opened it to serve the style of food we wanted to eat and we've done the same this time," Peter explained. "So if Nicola and I and the children are going out we generally end up having dumplings or similar, so that was the driving force."

But they didn't drop the baton at Caveau. Not even a fire that destroyed the kitchen in 2015 broke their run of hats. While both places were running, chefs Simon Evans and Tom Chiumento looked after Caveau and, after its 12th hat, the pair decided to buy the restaurant from the Sheppards. The couple had also decided to close down MoChi to pursue something different.

The change of ownership didn't mean a thing for the hats, which kept coming in 2018 and 2019. The only thing that was able to stop the 15-year run of hats was a global pandemic. In May 2020, while social distancing restrictions meant restaurants could reopen for up to 10 people. Chiumento and Evans decided to wait for the second stage in the easing of restrictions before they'd start serving again. But those doors wouldn't open again – coronavirus saw to that.

"Simon and I have poured everything we have had during the last few years into it," Chiumento said. "We were working north of 80 hours most weeks. We signed up for that. But then COVID completely ruined us and made it completely not feasible for us to be able to continue, which is really sad."

But Keira Street wasn't left without a hatted restaurant for long. In 2022 Babyface Kitchen earned a hat and kept it the following year.

Bar battle

If you stand on the northwestern corner of Keira and Crown streets and look to the west, you'll see a building that was the flashpoint in the city's changing drinking culture. A culture that was, for a long time, dominated by "meat markets frequented by cashed-up bogans", as local music historian Warren Wheeler so aptly put it.

What you'd be looking at from that Keira Street corner would be Humber, a bar that took its name from the original inhabitants of the building – Hillman Humber (a car retailer eventually taken over by Harrigan). It should be said that Humber wasn't the catalyst for a change in the way the city drinks. There had been a move away from the pubs and clubs for some time, prompted by the trickle of small bars opening up, like Otis, The Little Prince, His Boy Elroy and Dagwood.

That was due in part to Wollongong City Council's serious efforts to boost the night-time economy, along with an increase in the number of apartment towers going up. The people in those apartments needed places to go out at night, which prompted more places to open. What made the case of Humber a focal point was that the public spoke out about the new direction the city was taking – and they liked it.

In 2014 Adam Murphy was at the tail end of turning the building into a three-storey café and bar. The kitchen was on the ground floor, a main bar on the first floor and also a rooftop bar. "It's going to be very different to anything that's been in Wollongong before," Murphy said in October of that year. "The fit-out alone is worth around a million dollars and the base building works is another million."

The plan was to open the kitchen/café towards the end of October and the bars a month later. But that didn't happen; the Office of Liquor, Gaming and Racing (OLGR) was recommending to the Independent Liquor and Gaming Authority (ILGA) that Humber's liquor licence be knocked back. The reasons given were an apparent rise in alcohol-related violence and that there were already too many bars in the city.

It was a similar story to that heard by the Sifters shipping container café in nearby Market Street. The owners wanted to turn it into a bar but that was knocked back. The objections then included that Wollongong had "alcohol-related assault and offensive behaviour rates well above the state average, indicating the suburb does have an adverse concentration of alcohol-related anti-social behaviour".

But while the Sifters knockback seemed to come and go, the Humber case was a line in the sand for

Keira Street

Wollongong people. The Lord Mayor Gordon Bradbery came out in support of Humber, noting that the city's drinking culture had changed massively since he was a police chaplain in the late 1990s.

"I can remember virtual riots outside the Illawarra Hotel in Wollongong and violence on the streets of Wollongong," Cr Bradbery said. "We have better behaviour of patrons because we have lessened that bogan pub culture and are heading in the direction of more sophisticated drinking and responsible service of alcohol."

Destination Wollongong boss Mark Sleigh pointed to all those high-rises. "That potential residential capacity – which is quite a fundamental change to the city – is really driving the need for more of these bars." Yous and Owls' Ben Tillman said it was the nightclubs already in the city that "are giving hotels a bad name in general, because think about a place like Hobart where the pubs are amazing, or Melbourne's hotels".

And then there was Wheeler and his "cashed-up bogans" comment. Wheeler wasn't a fan of those people "whose primary goal on a Saturday night is to pre-fuel, hit the nightclubs and either provoke a fight or conquer a sexual desire (or both) sufficient enough to be able to regale their gym buddies with their tales of unsurpassed machismo the following morning."

But it wasn't all one-way traffic, with one of the city's top licencing cops saying the equation of 'more bars equals less violence' didn't add up. Relieving Southern Region licencing co-ordinator acting Senior Sergeant

Gary Keevers was commenting on a steady reduction in the rates of alcohol-related violence in the city. While others were keen to say the rise of small bars were the reason, Sgt Keevers wasn't buying it.

"It's my view that in any CBD, the introduction of more small bar licences will not contribute to a reduction in alcohol-related crime, it just simply will not," Sgt Keevers said.

"The number of assaults in Wollongong are definitely coming down but we need to make sure they are always on a downward trajectory. The sale and supply of alcohol is still the major contributor to these assaults around the state – and no matter what the type of venue, there is still the sale and consumption of alcohol."

Come February 2015, the liquor licence for Humber still wasn't forthcoming, though a public forum was held where all of the community speakers backed the proposal. That seemed to be a surprise to the OLGR executive director Paul Newson, who had attended the meeting.

"I attend many forums and I can tell you that none of them have had a collective voice that has been sponsoring a liquor application," he said.

"We've heard from the Lord Mayor, we've heard from the [police] local area commander and we've heard from the average citizen and there's been a uniform voice that has been encouraging of this venue and I think it's appropriate that we acknowledge that."

Mr Newson's other comments, suggested the ice may have been thawing around the Humber application. He noted that it was true that a mix of venues could have a positive impact. "There is absolutely a cumulative impact, but every licence does not have the same effect. A café, restaurant or a small bar has a very different effect to a large hotel or a traditional booze barn."

A month later, in March 2015, the licence came through. "It has been a long road to get to this point but we have always felt supported by the people of the city in our journey," Murphy said.

But the bars wouldn't open straight away; there was a two-month wait while Humber got all its ducks in a row. The first beers were pulled on May 15, at a special invite-only event. And Murphy didn't think the hunger for more and different bars had been satisfied with Humber's opening. "I don't think we're anywhere near saturation point," he said. Murphy would prove that himself; going on to open two more venues on Crown Street – Heyday and Halfway.

Bibliography

Alexakis, Effie, and Janiszewski, *Greek Cafes and Milk Bars of Australia*, Halstead Press, 2022

Apter, Jeff, *Johnny O'Keefe: Rocker, Legend, Wild One*, Hachette, 2013

Birchmeier, John, *A Time and Place: The Dion Family in 20th Century Wollongong*, published by John Birchmeier, 2019

Cossins, Annie, *The Baby Farmers*, Allen & Unwin, 2013

Fleming, AP, *The Albert Memorial Hospital*, Illawarra Historical Society, 1983

Hagan, Jim and Wells, Andrew (eds), *A History of Wollongong*, University of Wollongong Press, 1997

Humphries, Glen, *Alive In The Five: The Steelers 1992 Premiership Charge*, Last Day of School, 2024

Humphries, Glen, *Lull City: The Wollongong Music Scene 1955-2020*, Last Day of School, 2021

Irving, Robert, *Twentieth Century Architecture in*

Keira Street

Wollongong, Wollongong City Council, 2001

Keira Street also draws on the excellent work of my *Illawarra Mercury* colleagues – along with many others back in the days before newspaper bylines – and who have been tracking the changes along Keira Street for years

Veronica Apap
Alex Arnold
Hilary Blackwell
David Braithwaite
Anne Bransdon
Tess Brunton
Josh Butler
Lisa Carty
Mario Christodoulou
Brett Cox
Brendan Crabb
David Crayshaw
Grace Crivellaro
Graham Davis
Jenny Dennis
Jodie Duffy
Gabrielle Dunlevy
Greg Ellis
Geoff Failes
Antony Field
Nalita Ferraz
Dominic Geiger

Paddy Ginnane
Sam Hall
Edgar Hotan
Jessica Hough
David Iliffe
Carol Johnstone
Matthew Jones
Ben Langford
Kate McIlwain
Paul McInerney
Cydonee Mardon
Jodie Minus
Eileen Mulligan
Connor Pearce
Andrew Pearson
Brenna Quinlan
Bob Quintrell
Laurel-Lee Roderick
Tina Sorenson
Emma Spillett
Tom Sturrock
Angela Thompson
Shannon Tonkin
Ashleigh Tullis
Louise Turk
Michele Tydd
Lisa Wachsmuth
Kate Walsh
Michelle Webster

If you liked this book why not check out some of my others? For more information visit my own micropublishing company Last Day of School, which you'll find at www.lastdayofschool.net

Glen Humphries

Aussie Rock Anthems
The Stories Behind Our Biggest Hit Songs
Published by Gelding Street Press

What a famous song is about and what you think it's about aren't always the same thing. National Anthems names the top 40 classic Australian songs and tells the stories behind them - many unknown.

From Hunters and Collectors' *Throw Your Arms Around Me* to INXS' *Don't Change* and Redgum's *I Was Only 19*, this book unearths hidden gems and surprising back stories about the bands. It's a celebration of great Australian music that will have you reaching for old vinyl or phone apps to give some of these classics another listen. Chances are, each song is not what you had assumed.

"With Aussie Rock Anthems, Glen has written the perfect companion to the soundtrack of our lives."
Jeff Apter, author of High Voltage

Keira Street

Sticky Wickets
Australian cricket's controversies and curiosities

Published by Gelding Street Press

The story of cricket is littered with big stories, like Bodyline, underarm balls and tycoons changing the game. But, like Tony Greig checking out the pitch with his keys, sometimes things fall through the cracks.

Sticky Wickets takes a look at stories both big, small and perhaps forgotten. From bees and their dislike of cricket to a storm caused when a cameraman criticised a Test player's fielding. It's perfect to pick up when rain delays play.

Jack Gibson's Fur Coat Rugby League Artefacts and Oddities

Published by Gelding Street Press

If rugby league buried a time capsule Jack Gibson's fur coat would be the first item placed inside - if you could solve the mystery of its whereabouts.

League's precious artefacts include Thurston's headgear, Langland's white boots, Reggie the Rabbit's tail and a snag from the Dragons' season-ending BBQ. Or you could fill it with stories of players who were poisoned, didn't show for the grand final or took the field drunk.

Jack Gibson's Fur Coat tells the stories that live on the margins. You simply couldn't make up rugby league's best yarns.

Keira Street

Biff
Rugby League's Infamous Fights

Published by Gelding Street Press

For close to a hundred years, the biff has been part and parcel of rugby league. And it was condoned for most of that time. As rough play like stiff arms, high tackles, spear tackles, facials and stomping were weeded out of the game, the punch remained. As recently as the 1980s league bosses would say there was nothing fans liked to see more than two forwards trading blows.

But the biff has all but disappeared in recent years, when the league finally realised there is nothing in the rule book that allows players to punch on. *Biff* looks at some of the most infamous brawls in rugby league, from the Earl Park Riot and a match abandoned after it became a brawl to the most violent grand final and, finally, the punch that changed everything.

Friday Night at the Oxford

The story that led to reunion of legendary band Tumbleweed. An in-depth look at Sunday Painters, a band decades ahead of their time. Iconic shows like HOPE, HyFest and the Steel City Sound exhibition. These are just of the more than 100 stories about Wollongong bands and events written by journalist Glen Humphries for the *Illawarra Mercury*, from 1997 through to 2018, and his own short-lived website Dragster. The 200-plus pages of *Friday Night at the Oxford* provide a snapshot of what happened in the Wollongong music scene over the last 20-odd years – the bands, the venues, the events. It's a celebration of the music of a city.

So dig it.

Healer:
The Rise, Fall and Return of Tumbleweed

With their long hair and fuzzed-up guitars, Tumbleweed rose out of the ashes of late-80s indie band The Proton Energy Pills.

The Wollongong band hit their peak of popularity in the wake of the 1995 album *Galactaphonic*. And then proceeded to shoot themselves in the foot. Guitarist Paul Hausmeister got the sack, and then drummer Steve O'Brien left in protest. From there the band went downhill, releasing albums that met an increasingly uninterested public and playing shows in front of a half-dozen people. So it was no surprise when they called it quits in 2001.

But in 2009 they managed to heal their wounds and reunite, releasing their fifth studio album a few years later and survive the sudden death of bassplayer Jay Curley.

Journalist and music writer Glen Humphries has interviewed the members of Tumbleweed numerous times and, in Healer, takes the first complete look at the band's career.

Glen Humphries

Sounds Like an Ending: Midnight Oil, 10-1 and Red Sails in the Sunset

In 1982, Midnight Oil was a band in trouble. Their last album, *Place Without a Postcard*, was meant to be their breakthrough but it hadn't worked out that way. So they found themselves in London, feeling the pressure of recording what was a "make or break" album.

Out of the crisis came *10,9,8,7,6,5,4,3,2,1*, an album that changed everything for the band. It entered the charts and stayed there for more than three years. They started playing bigger venues – and they were able to pay back the bank manager.

Two years later, they headed to Japan to record the polarising *Red Sails in the Sunset*. It managed to do what *10-1* couldn't – give the band their first No1 album. *Sounds Like an Ending* takes a track-by-track look at these two albums and the times and turmoil that fuelled them.

> *"Intelligent, insightful and at times drily amusing.*
> Stuart Coupe, author of *Shake Some Action*

Alright! Queen at Live Aid

On July 13, 1985, the world tuned in to watch Live Aid beamed in from Wembley in London and John F Kennedy Stadium in Philadelphia. The massive event was spawned from Bob Geldof's idea six months earlier to raise money for Ethiopian famine victims through the release of the charity single, *Do They Know It's Christmas?*.

The iconic performance on that day came from Queen, a band that had been considering calling it quits just months earlier. Performing in front of an estimated audience of 1.9 billion people, the fourpiece stole the show and revitalised their career.

Alright takes a look back at Queen's performance on that day as well as revisiting the origins of the Band Aid single and the logistics behind getting Live Aid off the ground.

Glen Humphries

Little Darling
Daryl Braithwaite and The Horses

Most musicians only get one chance at fame. Daryl Braithwaite has managed to have three of them. He joined a band called Sherbet in 1970 and, a year later, they had their first hit - and there were an astonishing 19 more to come.

But Sherbet's fans grew up and moved on so the band folded in the early 1980s. At the end of that decade, Braithwaite found himself with a surprise hit album in *Edge*. He followed it up a few years later with *Rise* - the album that included a little tune called *The Horses*. That song went to No1, but a lawsuit and diminishing sales saw him pushed out of the limelight.

Then, in the early 2000s, something strange happened – kids at gigs started singing *The Horses* back at Braithwaite. Soon enough, this song that might have otherwise faded away galloped back and became an Australian anthem. *Little Darling* looks at the unusual phenomenon of *The Horses* and offers up an explanation for how it happened.

Keira Street

The Slab:
24 Stories of Beer in Australia

Beer. You know it and, chances are, you love it. But you might not know the part beer has played in Australian history. Right from the start beer was there. It was on board The Endeavour when Captain Cook set sail for Australia. It was drunk not long after the First Fleet landed in Botany Bay.

It was there when World War I soldiers got a skinful and ran riot in the streets of Sydney. It was there during the era of six o'clock closing where people were still drinking it long after the little hand had passed the six. It was even there when it really shouldn't have been - when Canberra declared itself an alcohol-free zone.

"History as it should be written. With beer. About beer. Crisp. Refreshing. Won't cause bloat."
John Birmingham, author of Leviathan

Glen Humphries

James Squire: The Biography

After getting caught swiping a few chickens from a neighbour, James Squire was sentenced to seven years in Sydney Cove. You could say it was the best thing he ever did – it led to him become a brewer, policeman, property tycoon, respected citizen and a bloody rich guy.
But if all you know about James Squire is what you've read on labels on beer bottles, then you really don't know that much at all.

This book – the first biography of Squire – separates the facts from the well-known myths. Along the way you'll also discover a few other things about Sydney Cove, including Captain Arthur Phillip's efforts to get his hands on some Aboriginal heads for a friend, the early Australian fondness for cider rather than beer, the fight rival brewer John Boston had over a dead pig and the marine who tried to trade his hat for an Aboriginal child.

Keira Street

Night Terrors: The True Story of the Kingsgrove Slasher

Between 1956 and 1959, suburban Sydney was terrorised by a phantom known as the Kingsgrove Slasher. A peeping Tom, he graduated to breaking into houses to watch people sleep before later slashing women and girls with a razor while they lay in their beds.

He punched a 21-year-old woman into unconsciousness, breaking her teeth and cutting her mouth, hit a teenage girl in the face with a piece of wood and slashed a deep wound across the stomach of a 64-year-old woman. The Slasher also groped teens in their beds, and one of his 18 victims was just seven years old.

Night Terrors is the first detailed account of the Kingsgrove Slasher case. It draws on hundreds of newspaper articles written at the time - which show the level of fear in the community - as well as the transcripts from the court hearings, which had been sealed since 1959.